Praise for *Word on Fire*

"Robert Barron has a unique talent for combining scriptural exegesis with a thorough knowledge of theology, both traditional and modern, the enterprise further undergirded by a firm grasp of philosophy. Barron uses this considerable technical apparatus in the service of homilies which are deeply religious and accessible to the average reader. Written in a clear and lively style, *Word on Fire* delivers homilies with panache. Highly recommended."

— Howard P. Bleichner, SS

"Robert Barron's reflections on the Scriptures weave vast learning, beautiful prose, and his own vivid faith into a seamless whole. First given as homilies, they are, for the reader, authentic meditations written by an engaging and learned younger priest theologian. A model for the preacher, these pages are solid food for everyone in the household of the Faith."

— Lawrence S. Cunningham, John A. O'Brien Professor of Theology, University of Notre Dame

"Robert Barron is one of today's premier Catholic spiritual writers. His new book breaks open several key Scripture passages to help readers plunge more deeply into the mystery of God's presence in the Bible and in their own lives."

— James Martin, SJ, author of *My Life with the Saints*

"Here is Robert Barron's distinctive voice: substantive and imaginative, clear and challenging. His words help fan God's Word into flame, as he proclaims, 'Behold, the beauty of the Lord.'"

— Robert Imbelli, Boston College

"Robert Barron's *Word on Fire* makes clear that Jesus Christ matters, that our response to Jesus' question, 'But who do you say that I am?' determines every aspect of our lives. Confidently but without arrogance or triumphalism, Barron calls us to encounter Christ in all of his strange beauty and humble power, and to respond in conversion and mission. Spanning intellectual heights and daily realities, Barron writes from his knees so that we may arise and walk in the power of Christ."

— Christopher Ruddy, author of *The Local Church* and *Tested in Every Way*

WORD
ON
FIRE

Other Crossroad books
by Robert Barron

And Now I See . . . A Theology of Transformation

Heaven in Stone and Glass:
Experiencing the Spirituality of the Great Cathedrals

Thomas Aquinas: Spiritual Master

WORD
ON
FIRE

PROCLAIMING THE
POWER OF CHRIST

ROBERT
BARRON

ILLUSTRATIONS BY
MICHAEL O'NEILL MCGRATH

A Crossroad Book
The Crossroad Publishing Company
New York

08|09

The Crossroad Publishing Company
16 Penn Plaza – 481 Eighth Avenue, Suite 1550
New York, NY 10001

Printed in the United States of America on acid-free paper

The text of this book is set in 12/17 Goudy Old Style.

Library of Congress Cataloging-in-Publication Data
Barron, Robert E., 1959-
    Word on fire : proclaiming the power of Christ / Robert Barron.
        p.   cm.
    Includes bibliographical references and index.
    ISBN-10: 0-8245-2453-5
    ISBN-13: 978-0-8245-2453-1
    1. Catholic Church – Doctrines.   I. Title.
    BX1751.3.B38 2008
    282 – dc22

                                                    2007052037

1 2 3 4 5 6 7 8 9 10   15 14 13 12 11 10 09 08

To
Srs. Domicela, Theodosia, and Cecelia:
faithful servants of the Lord

CONTENTS

Introduction: Lighting a Fire on the Earth   1

Part One
THE MYSTERY OF GOD

The Awful Holiness of God (Isaiah 6:1–8)   9

Giving God the Glory (1 Corinthians 10:31)   16

The Greatest Commandment (Luke 10:27)   22

Training in the Divine School (Hebrews 12:5–11)   28

Faith and Reason (Hebrews 11:1)   35

Part Two
JESUS THE CHRIST

Christ the King (John 18:33–38)   45

The Risen Lord (Mark 16:1–8)   51

Breaking, Singing, Pulling Away
(The Passion according to Mark)   58

Magi Came from the East (Matthew 2:1–12)   64

Contents

The Good Samaritan:
A Portrait of Christ (Luke 10:29–37)   70

The Mystery of Light (Matthew 17:1–8)   76

Part Three
LIFE IN THE SPIRIT

The Hymn to Love (1 Corinthians 13:1–13)   85

The Law of the Gift (Genesis 22:1–14)   92

The Ambitious Heart (Mark 10:35–45)   99

The Seven Gifts of the Holy Spirit (Isaiah 11:1–3)   105

A Living Sacrifice of Praise (Romans 12:1–2)   112

The Angels and the Beasts (Mark 1:12–13)   118

Part Four
HOLY MEN AND WOMEN

The Tax Collector's Conversion (Matthew 9:9–13)   127

Falling in Love with God (Luke 1:26–38)   134

Peter Maurin and Matthew 25 (Matthew 25:31–34)   139

Tu Es Petrus (Matthew 16:13–19)   146

Contents

Part Five
LITURGY AND PRAYER

The Mystery of the Mass (John 6:1–15)   155

The Rules of Prayer (Mark 11:20–25)   162

Real Presence (John 6:48–66)   169

Priest, People, and Rite (Revelation 4:1–11)   176

Part Six
FAITH AND CULTURE

Biblical Family Values (1 Samuel 1:9–28)   185

Being American, Being Catholic (Galatians 5:1)   191

"I Saw No Temple in the City. . . ."
(Revelation 21:22)   197

The Lessons of Nehemiah (Nehemiah 8:1–8)   203

"What Is Truth?" (John 18:37–19:11)   210

Ephphatha! (Mark 7:31–37)   216

Index of Names   223

Introduction

LIGHTING A FIRE
ON THE EARTH

PREACHING HAS ALWAYS been one of the greatest joys of the priesthood for me. Though I have, in the course of my ministry, proclaimed the word in front of hundreds of congregations and small gatherings, for the past seven years I have had the privilege of preaching to quite a wide audience through radio and the Internet. The essays that you are about to read are based upon those "radio" homilies. When I actually preached these sermons, I had a few pages of notes in front of me; for the sake of this book, I have translated the notes into more formal prose. I realize that some of my Protestant friends might smile at these comparatively brief "sermons," but they must remember that they were designed to fit within the Catholic liturgical context and hence to be no longer than about fifteen minutes. My hope is that, in this written format, the very brevity of the essays might make them a bit more digestible to the reader.

My whole life long I have been fascinated by the power of the spoken word. I can recall listening, when I was a young man, with rapt attention to the speeches of Martin Luther King Jr., John F. Kennedy, and Fulton Sheen. It was not only the content of their orations that compelled me, but also the very pitch and texture of their voices. King and Kennedy especially seemed to me to be singing rather than speaking their words. When I was a sophomore in high school, I was called upon to give a public speech in the context of English class, and I chose JFK's inaugural address, with its high rhetoric and distinctive cadences. As I spoke it in front of twenty or so of my classmates, I sensed (and to some degree participated in) the magic of it, and from that moment I knew that I wanted to be a public speaker. Through the grace of God, I've been able to fulfill that early aspiration precisely as a public speaker of God's holy word. I hope that some of the joy and oratorical excitement that I caught as a young man comes through in these sermon-essays.

But why should you bother reading these homilies? You should do so, because in the measure that they contain God's word, they contain the power to change you according to God's will. The authority of a real sermon comes, not from the preacher, no matter how eloquent, intelligent, or spiritually insightful, but rather from the

Holy Spirit. When I stand to homilize at Mass, I am wearing the formal vestments of a priest, highlighting the fact that my words are not so much mine as Christ's. If I were preaching my private opinions on the spiritual life, my congregation should give me about as much attention as they would if I were holding forth at a cocktail party. They should really attend to me precisely inasmuch as Christ is using me and my words to convey his word. So if it is Christ who speaks in these sermon-essays and if you take the time to listen, you will change. Commenting on the return of the Magi to their home country by another route after their visit with the child Jesus, Fulton Sheen said, "Of course they went back by a different road; no one comes to Christ and ever goes back the same way he came!"

When I was studying the art of preaching in the seminary, I took in a method that was all the vogue at the time. Rooted in Paul Tillich's theology, it advocated an experiential approach. We were encouraged to correlate general human experience to the symbols and doctrines found in the Bible, using the former as an interpretive grid for the latter. Only in this way, our teachers assured us, would we hold the attention of a skeptical modern audience. The result was that almost all of our homilies were long on stories and anecdotes and rather short on the Scripture. Sometime in the mid-1990s, I resolved to

teach a course on the Christology of the great preachers in the Christian tradition. Accordingly, I read the
sermons of, among others, Origen, Augustine, Bernard,
Thomas Aquinas, Meister Eckhart, Bossuet, Karl Barth,
and John Henry Newman. What struck me with a dis-
concerting clarity was that none of these masters of the
word used a correlational method, none of them employed experience as an interpretive grid for the Bible.
Rather, to a person, they allowed the biblical word to
seize them, to rearrange their thinking, to compel them
to ask different questions. Then they drew the world of
ordinary experience into the biblical world, interpreting
the former by means of the latter.

This realization effected a revolution in me, and I
began to preach differently, placing Christ first and my
own experience very much second. I learned to be patient with the Bible, allowing its distinctiveness and
oddity to come to the fore, resisting the temptation to
make it conform to cultural expectations and the contours of ordinary spiritual experience. Something else
that I learned from the preaching masters was the ample,
even exuberant, use of the Catholic tradition. Catholic
preachers do not subscribe to the reformation principle of
sola scriptura (by the Scripture alone); rather, they hap-
pily take advantage of the art, music, painting, poetry,

philosophy, saints' lives, and spirituality that serve as amplifications of the biblical message. Thus you will find in these sermons of mine much of that rich interpretive tradition.

Jesus said, "I have come to light a fire on the earth!" That fire was enkindled by the Lord's miracles, his healings, his dying and rising — and by his speech. My fondest hope is that some of the heat and light of Jesus' fiery word comes through the words of these simple homilies.

Part One

The Mystery of God

THE AWFUL HOLINESS
OF GOD
Isaiah 6:1–8

I N THE SIXTH CHAPTER of the book of the prophet Isaiah we find one of the most striking and illuminating biblical accounts of an encounter with God. As we've come to expect from the Scripture, this narrative is at the same time beautiful, puzzling, and deeply strange. We hear that Isaiah was in the temple when suddenly he "saw the Lord seated on a high and lofty throne, with the train of his garment filling the temple. Seraphim were stationed above. 'Holy, holy, holy is the Lord of hosts,' they cried to each other. 'The earth is filled with his glory.'" This vision occurs when Isaiah is in the temple precincts — perhaps even, as some scholars suggest, when he is in the holy of holies performing the high priestly function on the day of atonement. While he is praying in this sacred place, he *sees*. Here we learn something very important about the nature of prayer. Liturgy,

9

ritual, and prayer never draw God into our presence, the way magical incantations do. But they do dispose us to experience God's presence. Why would someone in Isaiah's time go to the temple every day to pray and offer sacrifice? Why would someone today engage in the rhythms of the liturgy of the hours or assist at daily Mass? They would do so in order to be ready and attentive when God chooses to disclose himself.

The Lord God allows himself to be seen, but how unnerving, paradoxical, and disorienting this vision is, in Isaiah's day and ours. Isaiah envisions God on a high throne, but he also remarks that the train of God's garment fills the temple. This play of transcendence and immanence, distance and closeness is typical in biblical descriptions of God. Adam and Eve, as we have seen, try to grasp at God, but they are confounded by God's ungraspable otherness; then they try to hide from God, but they are blocked by God's unavoidable closeness. Moses is drawn by the beauty of the burning bush but then is rebuffed when he tries to manipulate God by seizing his name. The sacred name, which is not a name — "I am who I am" — gestures toward this coincidence of transcendence and immanence in the God of Israel. The one who is must be beyond any of the particular things in the world, while at the same time he must be at the deepest ground of all created existence. "I am who I am" must be utterly mysterious and closer to us than we are to ourselves, and this means that the revelation of God is always, at the same time, the concealing of God. The fathers of the fourth Lateran Council caught this biblical idea nicely when they said that even as we affirm a similitude between the world and God, we should always simultaneously affirm a greater dissimilitude.

The cry of the seraphim, "Holy, Holy, Holy," which we echo at every Mass, indicates this unique form of God's difference. For biblical Israelites, "Holy" meant "set apart" or "absolute." God is set apart in a unique way, for his otherness is not a conventional otherness of spatial or metaphysical distance; it is an otherness that transcends and includes the distinction between ordinary distance and ordinary closeness. To use theologian Kathryn Tanner's phrase, God is "otherly other." And this uniquely divine strangeness is precisely what the angels are singing about.

I should like to linger with the angels a bit longer. The name "Seraph" designates "fire." These singers are, therefore, the members of the heavenly court who have caught fire because they attend so closely to the throne of God. They are like burning embers that carry some of the glow and heat of the fire that originally illumined them. "I am who I am" is not a particular existing thing but rather the source and ground of all of the perfection of existence. Thus, he is not so much a just *being* as justice itself, not so much a true thing as truth itself, not so much a good person as goodness itself. But good persons and true things and just beings reflect some of this divine intensity. They are, to varying degrees, angels or messengers of God. From the highest of the angels to ordinary rocks strewn along the floor of a quarry, all creatures are, in this sense, seraphim, on fire with the perfection of God. This is why acts of justice can transport us into the presence of the source of all justice; why decent people can bear us to that which is the source of all decency; why the perception of a truth, however basic, can trigger an experience of truth itself. Angels are everywhere, if we have the eyes to see.

Isaiah tells us that "at the sound of [the singing of the angels], the frame of the door shook and the house was filled with smoke." An experience of God always changes us; it never fails to shake the foundations on which we stand and rattle the walls that we trust will protect us. The true God, when he breaks into our lives, drives us out of our complacency, reconfigures us, knocks us to the ground. He is — to borrow just a few biblical images — a whirlwind, an earthquake, a conquering army, a thief in the night. Now why does Isaiah speak of smoke? Smoke not only obscures a visible object but also undermines the very act of seeing, causing a viewer to shut his eyes and blink back tears. "The one who is" cannot even in principle appear as an object to be studied, and his very presence confounds and frustrates every attempt to look, study, and analyze. This is why Joseph Ratzinger commented that Christian doctrines of God function at the intellectual level like the incense used at the liturgy: to some degree, they obscure the object to be known and frustrate the subject who tries to know.

After the vision, the angelic song, the shaking, and the smoke, Isaiah cries out, "Woe is me, I am doomed! For I am a man of unclean lips, living among a people of unclean lips." G. K. Chesterton observed that a saint is someone who knows that he is a sinner. He implies that the closer one gets to God, the more aware he becomes of his own sin, just as the spots and imperfections on a windshield appear more clearly when the sunlight shines directly on it. Isaiah's self-accusation in the presence of God is almost exactly echoed in the New Testament story of the miraculous draught of fishes. In the wake of the miracle, as it begins to dawn on him just who Jesus is, Peter exclaims: "Leave me, Lord, I am a sinful man." We are always humbled in the presence of the true God, convicted of our sin, less cocky and sure of ourselves. But this is all to the good, for what is being stripped away in that process is the false self, that perverted person who has compromised the image of God, the "man of unclean lips."

God listens to Isaiah's humble self-assessment, but he is not dissuaded by it. We hear that one of the seraphim flew to Isaiah and touched his mouth with a burning ember taken from the altar. The effect is a cleansing of Isaiah's soul: "Now that this has touched your lips, your guilt has departed and your sin is blotted out," says the Seraph. The God of Israel is not the least bit interested in awakening our sense of moral unworthiness so that we might wallow in it or so that he might feel superior by comparison. That might be a tactic of one of the mythological gods, but it is utterly alien to "the one who is." God wants us to acknowledge our sin (which we do inevitably when we stand in his presence), but then he wants to cleanse us and ready us for mission. "Then I heard the voice of the Lord saying, 'Whom shall I send? Who will go for us?'" No one in the Bible is ever given an experience of God without being, as a result, sent on a mission. Hence, Abram hears the voice of God and is immediately sent to discover the promised land; Jacob dreams of a ladder connecting heaven and earth and becomes, subsequently, the bearer of the covenant; Moses sees the burning bush and is told to liberate God's enslaved people Israel; Paul is knocked to the ground by the luminous presence of Christ and is commissioned as the Apostle to the Gentiles. The biblical God graces us with his presence that we might become missionaries of that presence to others.

And this is why theology is never, for Christians, a purely contemplative exercise. It always has a transformative and missionary purpose. And so this story of Isaiah's encounter with God ends, appropriately enough, with his ecstatic "Here I am! Send me!"

GIVING GOD THE GLORY

1 Corinthians 10:31

THERE IS A SNIPPET from Paul's first letter to the Corinthians that, with admirable concision, discloses the odd, counterintuitive logic at the heart of Christianity. The Apostle tells his little church at Corinth: "Whether you eat or drink — whatever you do — you should do all for the glory of God." Your whole life, he implies, should be ordered to the end of glorifying God and not your own egos. Now what precisely does Paul mean by "glory"? Behind the English term are the Greek word *doxa* (used, for example in the prologue to John's Gospel, "we have seen his glory") and the Hebrew word *kabod* (used to describe the glory of God that inhabits the temple in Jerusalem). The literal sense of both *kabod* and *doxa* would be something like "shine" or even "reputation." Therefore, to give God the glory is to allow God's light to shine, to advertise God, to draw attention to him — and away from ourselves.

16

But how difficult this is! From the time we are infants, we study the subtle art of glorifying ourselves, and over time most of us become quite adept at it. Most of our thoughts, moves, actions, and desires are subordinated to the great purpose of highlighting our own egos, drawing the spotlight selfward. And most of us, I imagine, would identify at least one feature of the good life to be *doxa,* that is to say, fame and good reputation. Paul is telling his company of fellow Christians that if they want to be disciples of Jesus, this tendency has to be reversed. The saint must live her life in such a way that her thoughts and actions draw attention to God's thoughts and actions. She must be, in accord with the metaphor of John of the Cross, a clear pane of glass through which the divine glory can shine.

Having heard this message, however, we face a dilemma, a conundrum that in fact was instrumental in the development of modern culture. Doesn't this principle articulated by St. Paul awaken in the human heart a sense of resentment? After all, why should God get *all* the glory? Are our achievements worth nothing? Do our legitimate accomplishments — moral, intellectual, technological, and scientific — not deserve at least some notice? Doesn't this talk of glorifying God at all costs indirectly denigrate the human project and lead in the direction of a sort of universal low self-esteem?

Many of the philosophers of the modern period wrestled with these questions and, under their weight, began to conceive of God as a rival to human flourishing, a reality that must, consequently, be marginalized or even eliminated altogether. Thus Deist thinkers such as John Locke, Thomas Jefferson, and Isaac Newton conceived of God as a power that, spatially and chronologically distant from the present world, allows the human project to unfold on its own, with only minimal interference. This Deist God, withdrawn into his radical transcendence, opened up a secular space, a playing field on which human beings could garner some glory of their own.

Now in time, even this diffident and distant God came to be seen by some theorists as a threat to human freedom. Ludwig Feuerbach, the greatest and most influential of the distinctively modern atheists, summed up his philosophy as such: "the no to God is the yes to man." Since, for Feuerbach, God is nothing but a projection of man's idealized self-understanding, humans will be liberated once they shake off the delusion of religious belief. Once the phantom of God gets none of the glory, then human beings can bask, rightfully, in the glory of their own heroic project. Feuerbach's most famous disciple was Karl Marx. As a young man, Marx was so impressed by Feuerbach's atheist philosophy that he said, "All of us must be baptized in the *Feuerbach*" (in German, "the fiery brook").

Furthermore, he insisted that all valid social and economic criticism must be preceded by Feuerbach's brand of religious criticism, for until men and women shake off the fundamental alienation of religion, they will not, he felt, be capable of dealing with more concrete forms of oppression. With his customary verve and pith, Marx gave voice to a fundamentally Feuerbachian sensibility when he famously commented, "Religion is the opiate of the masses," a drug that induces a dehumanizing stupor. Another massively influential thinker standing in the Feuerbach line was the founder of psychoanalysis. In his numerous writings on religion, Sigmund Freud characterized belief in God as an infantile illusion or a wish-fulfilling fantasy, a dream from which the human race ought to awaken. We want so desperately for there to be final justice, eternal life, a paradise where all human longing is satisfied, that we effectively invent the character of God, who will ground these hopes. Though comforting, this delusion effectively blocks real human progress. For Freud, as for Marx and Feuerbach, as long as we are giving God the glory, we are, in the most radical manner, undermining ourselves.

But this characteristically modern dilemma is born of a fundamental misunderstanding. The gods and goddesses of the pagan religions were indeed our rivals, for they needed something from us — our praise, our obedience, our flattery. But the God of the Bible stands in need of nothing, precisely because he is the creator of the universe in its entirety. The world neither adds nor subtracts anything from the perfection of God's being, and this means that God is utterly incapable of using, abusing, or manipulating the world for his purposes. As a consequence, God is something like a mirror which, upon receiving light from creation, reflects that light back for the illumination of the universe. To shift the metaphor: whatever we give to God breaks against the rock of God's self-sufficiency and returns to our benefit. This is why, if *God has no need,* it follows directly that *God is love.* Love is willing the good of the other as other. Since God has no need of anything, whatever he does and whatever he wills is purely for the sake of the other. The world, accordingly, is not a threat or rival to God — it is something which, in the purest sense of the word, has been loved into existence.

The god imagined by Freud, Marx, and Feuerbach is indeed involved in a desperate zero-sum game with the world: the more the god is elevated, the more the world is put down; the more the world is enhanced, the more the god is denigrated. But the true God, the "I am" who spoke to Moses out of the burning bush, the Lord who in overwhelming power confronted Isaiah in the temple, the God and Father of Jesus Christ — this

God is not party to such petty and pathetic competition with his creatures. Isaiah or Jeremiah or Ezekiel would have seen right through Feuerbach's fantasy and called it by its proper name — idolatry. And they would have gleefully turned Feuerbach's smug formula around: "the yes to God is the yes to man, and the no to God is the no to man." Authentic humanism does not negate God, but seeks relation to the true God, the one who needs nothing from us and can therefore use the glory that we give to him for our glorification. One of the greatest ironies of our time is that disciples of Feuerbach — Marx, Lenin, Stalin, Mao Tse-Tung, to name the most notorious — were the ones who, under the guise of freeing humans from their oppression, opened the door to the worst violations of human dignity in the history of the race.

Therefore, if you want real joy and authentic human flourishing, look not to the bitter scholarly arguments of modern atheists, but rather to the simple formula found in the first letter to the Corinthians: in all that you say and do, give God the glory!

THE GREATEST
COMMANDMENT

Luke 10:27

I T WAS A COMMON PRACTICE in Jesus' time to ask a rabbi to identify the central precept among the hundreds of laws that governed Jewish life, to specify the canon within the canon that would serve to interpret the whole of the Torah. Sometimes, to assure succinctness and brevity, a rabbi was compelled to offer this summary while standing on one foot. Thus Jesus, in accord with this custom, is asked, "Rabbi, which is the greatest commandment?" He gives his famous answer: "You shall love the Lord your God with all your heart, all your soul, and with all your mind. This is the greatest and first commandment. The second is like it: you shall love your neighbor as yourself."

All of religion is finally about awakening the deepest desire of the heart and directing it toward God; it is about the ordering of love toward that which is most worthy of love. But, Jesus says, a necessary implication of this love of God is compassion for one's fellow human beings. Why are the two commandments so tightly linked? There are many different ways to answer that question, but the best response is the simplest: because of who Jesus is. Christ is not simply a human being, and he is not simply God; rather, he is the God-man, the one in whose person divinity and humanity meet. Therefore, it is finally impossible to love him as God without loving the humanity that he has, in his own person, embraced. Therefore, the greatest commandment is an indirect Christology.

What does this entwined love of God and neighbor look like? To answer this question, we might turn, not first to the theologians, but to the saints. Rose Hawthorne was the third child of the great American writer Nathaniel Hawthorne, the author of *The Scarlet Letter, The House of the Seven Gables,* and some of the best short stories of the nineteenth century. Rose was born in 1851, when her father was at the height of his creative powers and enjoying a worldwide reputation. In the mid-1850s, Hawthorne, at the instigation of his friend President Franklin Pierce, was appointed U.S. consul to Liverpool, and the writer took his family with him to England. There Rose came of age in quite sophisticated surroundings. She studied with private tutors and governesses; she mixed and mingled with the leaders of

British society; and she traveled with her father to London, Paris, and Rome, where she even managed to charm Pope Pius IX.

But this idyllic existence ended rather quickly. Nathaniel Hawthorne died in 1864, when Rose was only thirteen, and her mother died just two years later, leaving the girl bereft and adrift. When she was twenty, she married a man named John Lathrop, and a few years later she gave birth to a son, whom she deeply loved. Her child died at the age of five, however, leaving his mother saddened, as she put it, "beyond words." At this time, her husband's alcoholism began to manifest itself, and their marriage fell on hard times. In her deep depression, Rose Hawthorne began a spiritual search that eventually led to an interest in Catholicism. Despite her family's rather entrenched Protestantism, she entered the Catholic Church.

A turning point in her life occurred when she read in the paper the story of a young seamstress of some means who had been diagnosed with cancer, operated upon unsuccessfully, and then told that her case was hopeless. Squandering her entire fortune on a vain attempt to find a cure, the woman found herself utterly destitute and confined to a squalid shelter for cancer patients. The story broke Rose's heart. Getting down

on her knees, she asked God to allow her to do something to help such people. In her prayer, the dynamics
of the greatest commandment were operative. Her compassion for suffering humanity led her to God, and the
confrontation with God led her to act on behalf of suffering humanity, the two loves joined as inextricably as the
divine and human natures in Christ. And God answered
her prayer. Rose enrolled herself in a nursing course and
began to work at a hospital specializing in the treatment
of cancer victims. On her first day at the hospital, she
met Mary Watson, a woman with an advanced case of
facial cancer, which rendered her so physically repulsive
that even experienced nurses and doctors balked at caring for her. But Rose didn't flinch. She helped to change
Mary Watson's dressing, and from that day they became
friends.

Rose rented a small flat on the Lower East Side of
Manhattan, living among the crowds of immigrant poor
who were flooding into New York at the time. (She and
her husband had separated, John having never been able
to get his alcoholism under control.) She simply opened
the doors of her apartment to cancer patients who had
nowhere else to go, and she cared for them. Mary Watson, cruelly discharged from the hospital by doctors who
considered her incurable, moved in with Rose. In time,
people came from all over New York to stay with her

and to find comfort in their dying days. And in accord with a basic law of the spiritual life, people began to present themselves as volunteers to help in Rose's work. We remember that when Francis of Assisi commenced to rebuild a crumbling church, he was soon joined by eleven helpers, and that when Mother Teresa of Calcutta went into the slums to aid the poor, she was joined by many of her former students. When people embrace God's work in a spirit of joy, others are drawn to them magnetically. Given the influx of patients and volunteers, Rose and her colleagues were obliged to rent larger space, which became possible because donations had begun to arrive.

At this point, Rose's husband, John, after a long and unsuccessful struggle with alcoholism, passed away, sending Rose into another bout of deep sadness. But his death also made possible what the Spirit was prompting her to do: to become a religious. She entered the Dominican order and took the name Sr. Mary Alphonsa. As a Dominican nun, she continued her work with cancer patients and in time managed to supervise the building of a large hospital in the country. Finally, with a number of other sisters, she formed a new branch of the Dominican order, dedicated specially to this much-needed and challenging work. This community of nursing sisters — now called the Hawthorne Dominicans — exists to this day and continues, with joyful devotion, to care for those suffering from incurable cancer.

Rose Hawthorne died in 1926. At the time of her death, her life story was published in a New York newspaper, where it was read by a young intellectual named Dorothy Day. Day was living on the Lower East Side and struggling to eke out a career as a journalist. She was also a spiritual seeker, and the encounter with Rose's story helped focus her energies and prompt her in the direction of a more radical love. Just a few years later, she founded the Catholic Worker movement, an organization dedicated to the intertwining of the love of God and the love of the poor, the hungry, the ignorant, and those forced to the margins of society. (We'll encounter Dorothy Day again, below.) A seed sown by Rose Hawthorne took root in the receptive soil of Dorothy Day's soul.

Those who know Christ Jesus, fully divine and fully human, realize that the love of God necessarily draws us to a love for the human race. They grasp the logical consistency and spiritual integrity of the greatest commandment.

TRAINING IN
THE DIVINE SCHOOL
Hebrews 12:5–11

IN THE YEARS FOLLOWING the Second Vatican Council — the time when I was coming of age in the church — teachers and preachers of the faith seemed to have an almost allergic reaction to any talk of divine punishment. If someone suggested that a suffering or a misfortune might have come as a punishment from God, he was deemed not only theologically misguided but ethically irresponsible. And there was, it seemed, good reason for this reticence. Didn't talk of divine punishment reek of a primitive religious consciousness? Didn't it place us within a more or less pagan framework, where the divine is understood as capricious and cruel? And hadn't this idea been stupidly and meanly employed over the centuries to assign guilt to those who were, in fact, innocent victims?

Yet the theme of God's punishment is one that can be found from beginning to end of the Bible — and not as a minor motif, but as a structuring element. Our very human condition, with its struggles, anxieties, and limitations, is understood by the book of Genesis as a chastisement for sin; the confusion of speaking different languages is, furthermore, construed as a punishment for man's hubris in building the Tower of Babel; the flood at the time of Noah is seen as resulting from the universality of human malice; the enslavement of the children of Israel, as well as their long wandering in the desert, is the bitter fruit of Israel's misbehavior. When Israel loses in battle, its defeat is invariably read as divine punishment; Saul's failure in his civil war against David is due to Saul's unfaithfulness to God's command; Eli's death is the result of his own sins and those of his two wicked sons; the death of David's son is the consequence of David's adulterous dalliance with Bathsheba; the division of Israel into a northern and southern kingdom is God's punishment, following from Solomon's infidelity to Yahweh; and the Babylonian captivity is, all the prophets agree, God's answer to Israel's disobedience.

Is this manner of theologizing an archaic peculiarity of the Old Testament? Let us consider just a few New Testament examples. Paul tells the Corinthians that many

of them are becoming sick and some are dying, precisely because they have not refrained from sacrificing
to idols. In the Acts of the Apostles, two people — Ana-
nias and Saphira — are struck dead because they disobey
the Apostles' order and keep their money and property
to themselves. And the book of Revelation — the last
book of the entire Bible — culminates in a vision of God
furiously chastising a sinful world. And these are just a
few examples, chosen at random from literally hundreds
of others throughout the biblical revelation. While all of
these texts are complex and multifaceted, we see from
the sheer multiplicity of these citations that it would be
deeply unbiblical to marginalize uncritically the category
of divine punishment.

A passage from the twelfth chapter of the letter to
the Hebrews is so clarifying and lucid in regard to the
question at hand that it can function as an interpretive key: "My sons, do not disdain the discipline of the
Lord nor lose heart when he reproves you; for whom the
Lord loves, he disciplines; he scourges every son he receives." At the heart of this statement is the correlation
of the divine punishment first to education and then to
love. What we find so objectionable in pagan accounts
is that the gods seem cruel and capricious in their chas-
tisements, as malicious and disproportionate as the worst
of earthly tyrants. But the Hebrews passage shows that

the biblical perspective is entirely different. God's punishment is always a disciplining born of love, a type of formation for the recalcitrant soul. And in the twelfth chapter, we find the perfect analogy for this divine behavior: "Endure your trials as the discipline of God who deals with you as sons. For what son is there whom his father does not discipline?" The governing metaphor for God throughout the Bible is that of parent — a good father or a good mother. The prophet Isaiah gives voice to Israel's deep conviction concerning the compassion of God in these lyrical words: "Would a mother forget her child? Yet even if she should forget, I will never forget you, my people. I have carved you in the palm of my hand." And Jesus himself addresses God with the endearment "Abba," a child's name for his loving father.

Do you know any good parent who does not, from time to time, discipline her child? Wouldn't it in fact be a sign of neglect or indifference if a parent never chastised, warned, or punished her daughter, never allowed her to feel the effects of her misbehavior, never warned him away from danger with a harsh word or glance? We all know about programs of "tough love," designed to encourage the parents of those who are in serious trouble with alcohol or drugs or violent behavior to help their children by making them directly experience the consequences of their misdeeds. Love is not a soft senti-ment; it is, as Dostoevsky said, "harsh and dreadful," precisely because it is the act of willing the good of the other as other. The mother who simply takes in a son mired in drug addiction, painlessly forgives him, and sets him back, without correction, on the path to self-destruction can hardly be described as a loving parent. And the father who allows his son to engage in reck-less sexual behavior, never providing any parameters for the young man or imposing any restrictions on him, is caring much more for his own ego than for his son's well-being. Thus God sometimes loves us in a harsh and dreadful way.

What is true of a single human family is true on a larger scale. The God who is the father of the universe has established, within creation, certain structures that reflect the integrity of his own being. Whenever we suc-cessfully move through a geometrical demonstration or conduct a scientific experiment or make a prudential moral decision, we are, at least implicitly, recognizing these structuring elements that God has set in place. If an inexperienced hang-glider willfully ignores the law of gravity, disaster results; and if an architect insufficiently appropriates the laws of geometry and physics, a build-ing may collapse. More to it, the abuse of the body — through overexertion, injury, or stress — results in pain;

and the misuse of the psyche leads to depression and anxiety. In none of these cases is the negative consequence the result of God acting arbitrarily; rather it is an indication of God's lawfulness. Now sin is nothing other than someone consciously contravening this divinely established order at the ethical level — and the divine punishment can be read, therefore, as God's allowing the sinner to experience the natural results of his contradiction of the moral fabric. It can be construed as God's tough love.

To be sure, those who are enduring God's chastisement rarely appreciate the contexts we have been suggesting, and the author of the letter to the Hebrews knows it: "At the time it is administered, all discipline seems a cause for grief . . . but later it brings forth the fruit of peace and justice to those who are trained in its school." The great church father Origen of Alexandria spoke often of the *schola animarum* (the school of souls), whose lessons begin now and reach their fulfillment only in the life to come. Our time on earth is a period of learning, refining, and purifying — something like an extended course or an athletic training program. Few really savor the day-to-day grind of education or the sweat and effort of football practice, but only a fool wouldn't see that pain is the condition for the possibility of progress in either arena.

We should not, however, draw the conclusion that any and all suffering can be interpreted as divine chastisement. It is just that sort of simple-minded thinking that has led many to reject the category of God's punishment altogether. And a careful reading of the book of Job should immediately disabuse us of the idea that suffering is always the result of sin. If we are biblical people, however, we must appreciate that some types of suffering are indeed expressions of the tough love of God and are indeed indications that we are undergoing training in the divine school.

FAITH AND REASON
Hebrews 11:1

P AUL TILLICH SAID that "faith" is the most misun-
derstood word in the Christian vocabulary. If that
assessment is true, we Christians are in some serious
trouble, for faith stands at the very heart of our program.
Thomas Aquinas said that faith is the door that gives
access to the divine life. Without it, neither the church,
nor the sacraments, nor the liturgy, nor the moral life
make any sense. Moreover, on the biblical reading, salvation history is nothing other than the journey in faith
undertaken by a series of figures from Abraham to Jesus
and beyond. If we're murky in regard to the meaning of
faith, that entire narrative becomes unintelligible.

So, what is faith? How should we understand this absolutely indispensable concept? A good place to start is
the eleventh chapter of the letter to the Hebrews, where
we find this definition: "Faith is confident assurance concerning what we hope for, the conviction of things not

seen." We glean from this description that faith is a straining ahead toward realities which are, at best, only dimly glimpsed. It is, necessarily, a walk in the darkness. But we also notice that faith is anything but a craven, hand-wringing, unsure business, for it is "confident" and marked by "conviction" and "assurance." Consider for a moment great figures of faith from Jacob and Joseph to Mother Teresa and John Paul II: these are hardly people that you'd be tempted to characterize as vacillating and unclear in their motivations. For faith, there is always a paradox of obscurity of vision and strength of purpose.

It is this paradox that the philosophers of modernity couldn't bear. They tended to see reason alone as the legitimate ground for confidence, and so they saw a resolute faith as a species of foolishness or irrationality. The English philosopher John Locke gave pithy expression to this typically modern sense when he said that there should be a tight relationship between inference (cogent argument) and assent (acknowledging something to be true). If these two moves of the mind are separated — as they seem to be in people of faith — obscurantism and fanaticism follow. It is fascinating to note how often, in the wake of the events of September 11, this Lockean argument has been reproposed. In the face of the dangers of religious extremism, many commentators are saying, give us cautious and skeptical people of reason rather than superstitious people of faith, willing to act with utter conviction despite the lack of any compelling evidence.

Are we simply at an impasse, then, between faith and reason? Does the definition of faith in the letter to the Hebrews hook us on the horns of a hopeless dilemma? One of the most insightful explorers of the relationship between faith and reason was John Henry Newman, and in many ways, his work in this area was an attempt to expose Locke's modern dilemma as false. Newman was writing at a time — the mid-nineteenth century — when the Christian churches were coming under withering attack from philosophers, social theorists, and especially scientists. Newman's rejoinder to the critics of Christianity was a subtle form of what the logicians call a *tu quoque* (you do it, too) argument. In his masterpiece *The Grammar of Assent,* Newman showed how even the most ordinary forms of reasoning involve something akin to faith. Why, to use Newman's famous example, does someone claim that England is an island? He does so on the basis of a collection of pieces of evidence from a wide variety of sources, very few of which could be directly or empirically verified. He has to consult maps (the accuracy of which he must take on faith); he has to read books of history (whose testimony he must take on faith); he has to listen to a host of other people (some or all of whom could be lying). In this process of coming to assent in the matter of England's insularity, reason is certainly in play, but it is by no means the only player. Hunch, intuition, trust, hearsay, and faith are all ingredient. And so it goes with any act of intellection, save the most banal of mathematical calculations. In a word, assent, even in this simple matter, is not simply reducible to inference. And Newman's keenest insight is this: despite the lack of totally convincing inferential support, the person who claims that England is an island is not the least bit hesitant or vacillating in his claim. He makes it, on the contrary, with utter confidence. So, he implies, does the man of faith combine lack of surety and strength of conviction.

One of Newman's best-known twentieth-century disciples was the Canadian Jesuit Bernard Lonergan. Lonergan demonstrated that every scientist relies upon faith, precisely in the measure that she assumes the accuracy of huge amounts of material — from the multiplication tables, to the value of pi, to the trajectories of projectiles, to the periodic table of elements — she does not directly verify. And moreover, something like faith is at the bottom of any scientific enterprise. Every great intellectual searcher, from Aristotle to Newton to Einstein, is lured in his knowing by what he doesn't know, by the intriguing darkness that stretches out ahead of him. Einstein, for example, dedicated the last years of his life to finding a unified field theory that would bring together the data and conclusions of all of the major physical sciences. Did he know that there was such a coherent, all-embracing theory? No, but he intuited it and allowed himself to be directed by it.

What all of these observations and examples indicate is that the line between faith and reason is not nearly as sharp as the avatars of the Enlightenment thought. In fact, if Newman and Lonergan are right, religious people and scientific people think in fundamentally similar ways, through a blend of belief and strict calculation. Therefore, we should not place religion and science on opposite sides of some great divide, but rather see them as modes of knowing that, despite their obvious differences in object and method, share a deep family resemblance. How do reasonable people come to believe in God? In much the same way that they come to convictions about matters geographical or chemical or historical — that is to say, on the basis of experiences, deductions, arguments, testimonies, and gut feelings. Thus there are rational demonstrations for God's existence based upon the radical contingency of the world (Thomas Aquinas's "five ways" are prime examples of these); God's existence can also be intuited directly through the witness of the conscience (Newman developed an argument along these lines); there is the long and steady witness of inspired figures over the centuries (especially as recounted in the Sacred Scriptures); and many have their own personal experiences of God. Perhaps none of these is absolutely convincing in itself; perhaps all could be quarreled with or explained away. Yet when all of these arguments, intuitions, and experiences converge on the same point, the mind is moved to assent. Newman referred to this instinct of the mind for the coherence of probable evidences as the "illative sense," implying that it carries (*latus*) the intellect to assent. One thin cable might not be enough to lift a great weight, but fifty such cables wrapped tightly around one another could easily get it off the ground. In the same way, any single argument or feeling or hunch would not be enough to move the mind to assent in the matter of God's existence, but five or ten or fifty of them would be more than enough to do so.

Thus we can conclude that the description of faith in the letter to the Hebrews is coherent. Like all forms of knowing, faith will involve a certain groping in the darkness, an ordering toward things unseen, an element of nonrationality. In fact, these features will be exaggerated in relation to faith, since it is directed to the ultimately mysterious reality of God. However, none of this precludes assurance in the person of faith, any more than the nonrational dimension of scientific or historical knowledge precludes confidence in the scientist or historian. Therefore, just as Einstein was motivated by an epistemic ideal he only barely glimpsed, so the faith-filled person is lifted up, guided, and inspired by that most alluring of unseen realities, the Lord God.

Part Two

Jesus the Christ

CHRIST THE KING

John 18:33–38

O NE OF THE EARLIEST and most basic forms of Christian proclamation is this: *Iesous Kyrios* (Jesus is Lord). We tend to think of this claim in "religious" terms, as an indication that Jesus is Lord in a spiritual sense, and it does indeed carry such a meaning. But when the first Christians used the phrase, it had a provocative political overtone as well. For in the ancient world, in the lands surrounding the Mediterranean, Caesar was the Lord, the one to whom ultimate allegiance was owed. *Kaisar Kyrios* (Caesar is Lord) was a watchword of the time and a proof of loyalty. In saying, therefore, that Jesus is *Kyrios*, they were directly challenging Caesar and all of the powers that operated under his aegis and in his name. It should not be too surprising then that Paul spent much of his ministry in jail and that (with the exception of John) all the Apostles were martyred and that the church was for three centuries periodically beset by brutal persecution. The enemies of the faith clearly understood what was entailed in the boast that someone crucified by Caesar was in fact the Lord. Ours has been, from the beginning, a troublemaking faith.

Political rulers come across in the New Testament about as well as they do in the Old Testament — which is to say, not very. In Luke's Christmas account, Caesar Augustus is implicitly compared unfavorably to the Christ child, the newborn king. Herod, the king of the Jews, is so desperate and self-absorbed that he hunts down that same child, killing innocent children in a vain attempt to stamp out his rival. Later, Herod's son, Herod Antipas, persecutes both John the Baptist and Jesus himself, and Jewish political/religious leaders are presented in all of the Gospels as vain, corrupt, and violent. (Nicodemus and Joseph of Arimathea are rare exceptions.) And the public career of Jesus comes to a climax when the Lord confronts Caesar's local representative, the crafty and self-regarding Pontius Pilate. Despite some attempts to romanticize him as a tortured but well-meaning man, Pilate was a fairly typical Roman governor: coldly efficient, concerned with good order, and, when necessary, brutal. He once put down a rebellion by nailing hundreds of Jews to the walls of Jerusalem. And like so many of the other political rulers of that time and place, he quite correctly perceived Jesus as a threat.

In John's version of the story, when Pilate stands face to face with Jesus, he asks: "So you are a king?" Jesus answers evasively, for he knows what Pilate means by "king": one more earthly ruler obsessed with power and all too willing to use violence to preserve it. Then he adds: "My kingdom does not belong to this world." We have to be careful in interpreting this observation, because there is always a double meaning to the term "world" in the Gospel of John. On the one hand, "world" designates the universe that God has created and which he sustains in love. This is the world that God loved enough to send his only Son as its savior. On the other hand, "world" means that manner of ordering things which is out of step with God's intentions; it indicates a political and cultural realm in which selfishness, hatred, division, and violence hold sway.

What Jesus implies, therefore, is not that his kingdom is irrelevant to ordinary experience, but that his way of ordering is radically out of step with the way practiced by Caesar, Pilate, Herod, and all the other usual suspects. In short, Jesus' kingdom has everything to do with "this world" in the first sense of the term and nothing to do with it in the second. Jesus continues: "If it were of this world, my subjects would be fighting to save me from being handed over to the Jews." *The* mark of the worldly kingdom is violence and the maintenance of order through force and fear. Though it is counter-intuitive in the extreme, and unrealistic, to say the very least, Jesus' reign will eschew all such means. It will suffer injustice, but it will not perpetuate it. These dynamics of Jesus' kingdom are on full display in the events of Good Friday. Christ the King is crowned and he assumes his throne, but the crown is made of thorns, and the throne is a Roman instrument of torture. In a supreme irony, it is Pilate himself who announces to all the world, in Hebrew, Latin, and Greek, Jesus' universal kingship. And from his royal place, Jesus speaks, not words of vengeance, but words of forgiveness, even to those who are killing him.

Three and a half centuries after the New Testament period, Augustine, the bishop of Hippo Regius on the North Africa seacoast and a man imbued with the best of Roman culture, wrote a book entitled *The City of God.* Heartbroken over the fall of Rome to northern barbaric tribes, this worthy literary successor of Cicero and Cato composed a sustained and vigorous attack on the empire he loved. From the establishment of the city to the present day, Augustine argued, Rome's power had been predicated upon violence and the oppression of the weak by the strong. Roman order was conditioned by a *libido dominandi* (a lust to dominate), which was in turn supported by the worship of violent, capricious, and deeply immoral gods. And this meant, he concluded, that the justice of Rome (trumpeted by its defenders as the very paragon of right order) was in fact a pseudo-justice, akin to the discipline and purposefulness one might find in a successful gang of robbers. Real order, Augustine continued, will come only when forgiveness, nonviolence, and the love of enemies are the regnant values — and only when these are supported by the worship of the true God who is, by his very nature, love. There is a direct line that runs from the New Testament to *The City of God*, for both present the contours of the new kingdom, and both pronounce judgment on the old.

Now, I would submit, this proclamation of the kingship of Jesus Christ poses a special challenge to us Americans. We are undoubtedly the dominant political and cultural power of the present day, and we are, still, a predominantly Christian country. This sets up a certain tension, to say the least. Even as we love our country (as Augustine surely loved Rome), we have to maintain that our loyalty to Christ is greater than our loyalty to the American political order. Reading it through the lenses provided by the Gospel, we must remain critical of the deep dysfunction of our society: the availability of abortion on demand, the growing acceptance of the legitimacy of euthanasia, the terrible violence on our city streets, the stockpiling of weapons of incomparable destructiveness, the waging of preemptive war, etc. Have we Christians accommodated ourselves too readily to the social and political structures? Have we effectively surrendered to the power of the world? One way to answer those questions is to ask two others: how many Christian martyrs are there among us? How many of us are in prison for our faith?

I have heard rather frequently over the years the suggestion that the Kingship of Christ is an outmoded idea, an image alien to our democratic sensibilities, and that, consequently, we should adopt the language of, say, Christ the President or Christ the Prime Minister. But this would be counterproductive. We have enormous control over presidents and prime ministers; they must stand regularly before the electorate and can, at the whim of the people, be put out of office. They must, to a large extent, pander to the shifting desires of those who choose them as representatives. We sinners would love just that kind of relationship with Jesus. A king, on the other hand, is one to whom total allegiance is due, one who is not subject to the people but who rather commands and orders them. If the way of Jesus is to prevail over and against the enormous power of the way of the world, he must be acknowledged as king and commander — and we must be willing to march in his army.

THE RISEN LORD
Mark 16:1–8

THE RESURRECTION is the be-all and end-all of Christian faith. It is the still point around which everything Christian turns. It is the great non-negotiable at the heart of our system of beliefs and practices. The four Gospels, the epistles of Paul and John, the writings of Augustine, Jerome, and Chrysostom, the poetry of Dante, the *Summa theologiae* of Thomas Aquinas, Michelangelo's Sistine Ceiling, Chartres Cathedral, the sermons of John Henry Newman, the mysticism of Teresa of Avila, the radical witness of Mother Teresa of Calcutta — all of it flows from the event of the resurrection, and without the resurrection, none of it makes a bit of sense. Paul stated this truth as succinctly and clearly as you could wish: "If Christ has not been raised, your faith is in vain." The resurrection of Jesus from the dead *is* the Gospel, the *euangelion*, the Good News. Everything else is commentary.

But what precisely do Christians mean when we speak of Christ's resurrection? Let me get at it indirectly, by specifying what we don't mean. Despite the suggestions of far too many theologians in recent years, we don't mean that "resurrection" is a literary conceit, a symbolic way of expressing the truth that Jesus' "spirit" or "cause" survives his physical demise. In the 1970s, Edward Schillebeeckx speculated that, after Jesus' terrible death, his disciples gathered together in their fear and pain for mutual support. What they discovered in time, largely through the suggestions of Peter, was that, despite their cowardly abandonment of Jesus at his hour of need, they "felt forgiven" by their departed Lord. They expressed this subjective experience through evocative narratives about an empty tomb and appearances of the risen Jesus. Only naïve readers, then and now, would take such stories as straightforward history, Schillebeeckx concluded. We find something very similar in the recent Christology proposed by Roger Haight. Haight speculates that the disciples came together after the death of Jesus and recalled, over time, his words, deeds, and gestures, and how Jesus had been for them a privileged symbol of the presence of God. This survival of the provocative memory of Jesus in their midst they expressed in the pictorial language of the biblical resurrection stories.

If that's all the church means by the resurrection of Jesus, I say, "Why bother?" This essay is too brief to adequately engage such a reductive mode of interpretation. But suffice it to say that were this approach correct, the language of resurrection from the dead could be applied, with equal validity, to practically any great religious or spiritual figure in history. Didn't the followers of the Buddha fondly remember him and his cause after his death? Couldn't the disciples of Confucius have sat in a memory circle and recalled how he had radically changed their lives? Couldn't the friends of Zoroaster have felt forgiven by him after he had passed from the scene? Indeed, couldn't the members of the Abraham Lincoln Society manage to generate many of the convictions and feelings about Lincoln that Schillebeeckx and Haight claim the apostles generated about Jesus? And would any of these demythologizing explanations begin to make sense of that excitement, that sense of novelty, surprise, and eschatological breakthrough that runs right through the four Gospels, through every one of the epistles, to the book of Revelation? Can we really imagine St. Paul tearing into Corinth with the earth-shaking message that a dead man was found to be quite inspiring? Can we really imagine St. Peter enduring his upside-down crucifixion because he and the other disciples had "felt forgiven"?

More to it, these painfully reductive readings of the resurrection stories actually betray a thin and unsophisticated grasp of the biblical authors. Here the magisterial work of the New Testament scholar N. T. Wright is particularly illuminating. Wright says that the composers of the New Testament were aware of a whole range of options in regard to the status of those who had died. From their Jewish heritage, they knew of the shadowy realm of Sheol and the sad figures that dwell therein. They knew further that people could return from Sheol in ghostly form. (Think of the prophet Samuel called up from the dead by the witch of Endor in the first book of Samuel.) They even had a sense of reincarnation, evident in widespread convictions about the return of Elijah in advance of the Messiah or in the popular report that Jesus himself was John the Baptist or one of the prophets returned from death. From the Hellenistic and Roman cultural matrix, furthermore, the New Testament authors would have inherited the Platonic theory that the soul at death escapes from the body as from a prison in order to move into a higher spiritual arena. They also were aware of a perspective, combining both Greek and Hebrew elements, according to which the souls of the dead abide for a time with God in a quasi-disembodied state, while they await the general resurrection at the eschaton. This view is on clear display in the famous passage from the book of

Wisdom that says, "The souls of the just are in the hand of God and no torment shall touch them." Finally, they knew all about hallucinations, illusions, and projections (though they wouldn't have used those terms), as is clear from the first reactions of the disciples upon hearing the reports of Jesus' postresurrection appearances.

The point is *that they used none of these categories when speaking of the resurrection of Jesus.* They didn't say that Jesus had gone to Sheol and was languishing there; nor did they claim that he had returned from that realm à la Samuel. They certainly did not think that Jesus' soul had escaped from his body or that he was vaguely "with God" like any other of the righteous dead. They did not think that the general resurrection of the dead had taken place. And most certainly, they did not think that the resurrection was a symbolic way of talking about something that had happened to them. Again and again, they emphasize how discouraged, worn down, and confused they were after the crucifixion. That this dejected band would spontaneously generate the faith that would send them careering around the world with the message of resurrection strains credulity.

What is undeniably clear is that something had happened to Jesus — something so strange that those who witnessed it had no category apt to describe it. Perhaps we would get closest to it if we were to say that what was expected of all of the righteous dead at the eschaton — bodily resurrection — had come true in time for this one man, Jesus of Nazareth, the same Jesus whom they knew, with whom they had shared meals and fellowship. This Jesus, who had died and had been buried, appeared alive to them, bodily present, though transformed, no longer conditioned by the limitations of space and time. This is what rendered them speechless at first and then, especially after the event of Pentecost, prepared to go to the ends of the earth, enduring every hardship even to the point of martyrdom, in order to proclaim the Good News.

The women came to the tomb early on Easter Sunday morning in order to anoint the body of Jesus and pay their respects. As they made their way to the sepulcher, they probably shared stories of Jesus and repeated his words, recalling to one another how profoundly he had influenced them. They undoubtedly expected to linger at the tomb after their task was completed, continuing to reflect wistfully and sadly on this great man. This is, more or less, what any mourners would do at the tomb of a fondly remembered friend. But there is nothing peaceful about the tomb of Jesus. When the women arrived, they noticed that the stone had been rolled away. Suspecting that someone had broken in and stolen the body, they approached the open grave, only — to their infinite surprise — to spy a man in a white garment who said "the one you seek is not here." It is at that moment that they began to suspect that someone, in fact, had broken *out* of the tomb. So overwhelmed, so disoriented were they that they ran from the spot — "frightened," Mark tells us, "out of their wits." Gathered round the tomb of a friend or hero, one might feel nostalgic, sad, inspired, but one would not, I suggest, be frightened out of one's mind. The point is this: something so new happened at Easter that the tame category of wistful remembrance is ludicrously inadequate as an explanation.

Jesus is risen; it is true. And that makes all the difference.

BREAKING, SINGING, PULLING AWAY

The Passion according to Mark

T HERE IS NO STORY better known to Western people than the narrative of Christ's passion and death. Whether we believe it or not, whether or not it plays a role in shaping our religious lives, this story is in our blood and our bones. Ernest Hemingway once related a story about a cabin boy on one of his boats who was reading a book with rapt attention. Hemingway asked the young man what he was studying so carefully, and he responded, "the Gospel of Mark." "Well, why," he continued, "are you so wrapped up in it?" And the boy said, "I'm dying to see how it ends!" The anecdote is funny, of course, because it's so anomalous: who, in the Western world, doesn't know how that most familiar of stories ends? But this very familiarity can block our appreciation of the dynamics of the passion narrative. Once this best-known of all stories gets under way, it can swim effortlessly through our minds, unfolding without really being noticed. What I wish to do therefore is to defamiliarize the account a bit by drawing your attention to three odd details in Mark's version of the passion, each one of which, precisely in its quirkiness, sheds light on the meaning of the text.

On Mark's telling, the passion narrative commences with the account of a woman who performs an extravagant act: "While he was at Bethany in the house of Simon the leper, as he sat at the table, a woman came with an alabaster jar of very costly ointment of nard, and she broke open the jar and poured the ointment on his head." This gesture — wasting something as expensive as an entire jar of perfume — is sniffed at by the bystanders, who complain that, at the very least, the nard could have been sold and the money given to the poor. But Jesus is having none of it: "Let her alone; why do you trouble her? She has performed a good service for me." Why does Mark use this tale to preface his telling of the passion? Why does he allow the odor of this woman's perfume to waft, as it were, over the whole of the story? It is because, I believe, this extravagant gesture shows the meaning of what Jesus is about to do: the absolutely radical giving away of self. There is nothing calculating, careful, or conservative about the woman's action;

she offers everything, breaking open the jar as a symbol of the breaking open of her heart in love. Giving voice to the austere rationalism of the Enlightenment, Immanuel Kant spoke of "religion within the limits of reason alone"; but as Paul Tillich commented, authentic religion, ultimate concern, can never be hemmed in by reason alone. Flowing from the deepest place in the heart, religion resists the strictures set for it by a fussily moralizing reason (on full display in those who complain about the woman's extravagance). At the climax of his life, Jesus will give himself away totally, lavishly, unreasonably — and this is why the woman's beautiful gesture is a sort of overture to the opera that will follow.

A second peculiar detail in Mark's account concerns the Last Supper and its immediate aftermath. Jesus has gathered with his intimate friends on the night before his death. He knows that the next day he shall be tortured and publicly executed. In the course of the supper, Jesus identifies himself so radically with the Passover bread and wine that they are now properly called his body and his blood. Like broken bread, the Lord says, his body will be given away in love; and like spilled wine, his blood will be poured out on behalf of many. The sadness and portentousness in that room must have been unbearable, much like the mood in the prison cell where a condemned man sits with his family while he awaits his execution. How does this terrible gathering come to a close? They sing! "After singing songs of praise, they walked out to the Mount of Olives." Can you imagine a condemned criminal blithely singing on the eve of his execution? Wouldn't there be something odd, even macabre, about such a display? But Jesus knows — and his church knows with him — that this joyful outburst, precisely at that awful time, is altogether appropriate. This is not to deny for a moment the terror of that night nor the seriousness of what will follow the next day; but it is to acknowledge that an act of total love is the passage to fullness of life. Therefore, as you give your life away, sing! Every Mass is a remembrance of that somber night: during the eucharistic prayer, we explicitly recall what Jesus did "the night before he died." But immediately after the consecration, as Christ in his sacrificial death becomes really present to us, we sing an acclamation of praise. The strange juxtaposition of terror and exuberant joy mimics the dynamics of the Last Supper.

A third peculiarity of Mark's version of the passion is the curious appearance of a naked man in the Garden of Gethsemane. In the confusion following the betrayal and arrest of Jesus, as the disciples flee their master, an unnamed youth finds himself in an awkward predicament: "A certain young man was following him, wearing nothing but a linen cloth. They caught hold of him, but he left the linen cloth and ran off naked." Scholars suggest that, like a Renaissance painter who places contemporary figures anachronistically into a depiction of a biblical scene, Mark is symbolically situating all of us in the Garden of Gethsemane in the figure of this man running off into the night. The principal clue to his symbolic identity is in the simple description "follower of Jesus," which makes him evocative of all disciples of the Lord from that day to the present. Another clue is his manner of dress. The Greek term here is *sindona,* which designates the kind of garment worn in the early church by the newly baptized. The point is this: following Jesus, being a baptized member of his church, is a dangerous business. Participating in Jesus' kingdom puts you, necessarily, in harm's way, for Jesus' way of ordering things is massively opposed to the world's way of doing so. The shame of this young man — running away from the Lord at the moment of crisis — is the shame of all of us fearful disciples of Jesus who, more often than not, leave behind, in the hands of our enemies, our baptismal identity. The naked young man, escaping into the night, therefore poses a question: what do we do at the moment of truth?

This mysterious figure makes a comeback before the Gospel of Mark closes, and in his return all of us sinners can find hope. On the morning of the resurrection, the

Marys come to the tomb, carrying their spices and fretting about the massive stone covering the mouth of the grave. They find the stone rolled away and, upon entering the sepulcher, they see "a young man dressed in a white robe, sitting on the right side." The words used for "young man" and "white robe" are the same that Mark used to describe the disciple in the Gethsemane scene. This confident figure announces the resurrection to the startled women. "Do not be alarmed; you are looking for Jesus of Nazareth who was crucified. He has been raised; he is not here." Exegetes suggest that this angelic presence in the empty tomb of Jesus is evocative of all of us disciples of Jesus at our best. Wearing once more our white baptismal garments, which we had abandoned during times of persecution, we announce to the world the good news that the crucified one is alive. Having recovered our courage, our voice, and our identity, we function as angels (the word *angelos* simply means messenger) of the resurrection.

An alabaster jar broken open and the smell of perfume filling the house; a songburst on the eve of execution; a humiliated man now become an angel. Three peculiar Markan lenses for reading the greatest story ever told.

MAGI CAME
FROM THE EAST
Matthew 2:1–12

A T THE END of the Gospel of Matthew, Jesus tells his disciples: "Go and preach to all nations, baptizing them in the name of the Father and of the Son and of the Holy Spirit." Very soon after his conversion experience on the road to Damascus, Paul resolves to become the Apostle to the Gentiles and, in accord with that resolution, he spends the rest of his life on a series of missionary journeys to distant lands. In his letter to the Galatians, Paul cries out: "In Christ there is no slave or free, no man or woman, no Jew or Greek," implying that the most basic features distinguishing human beings one from another are overcome in Jesus. Simon Peter, the humble fisherman from Capharnaum, ends his days in Rome, among Gentiles at the capital of the Roman Empire. Having heard these stories many times, we might take these sayings and deeds for granted today, but they are really quite extraordinary novelties for first-century Jews. Israelites considered themselves to be the specially chosen people of God, and the cultivation of their distinctive marks of belief — land, culture, and practice — was central to their sense of national and religious identity. To be sure, thoughtful Jews, following indications in the prophet Isaiah and in the psalms, knew that Israel's ultimate mission was to be a light to all the nations, but this was seen as an event in the distant eschatological future. This side of the eschaton, the sharp demarcation between Jew and Gentile was all-important.

But then something changed. Something so extraordinary happened that certain Jews began to act as though Isaiah's dream was coming true here and now. That something was the event of Jesus. From the earliest days of his life, Jesus was sought and extolled, not simply by Jews, but by representatives of the Gentile nations: we hear in Matthew's Gospel that "Magi from the East came to do him homage." Somehow these mysterious figures intuited that this child was more than just another king of Israel, more than another local potentate or tribal chieftain. They grasped (however inchoately) that this baby was more than a human figure and that, as a consequence, his coming was of significance for everyone. How wonderful it is that in most depictions of the Wise Men (about whom we know practically nothing), they are portrayed as men of differing racial backgrounds. This might not be historically accurate, but it rings true theologically, for there is something on offer in Jesus that is properly transnational and transhistorical. And in this universality is our hope.

Even the most cursory survey of world history reveals the havoc wreaked by hypernationalism and an obsession with ethnic and religious peculiarity. In the wake of the Reformation, wars between Catholics and Protestants ravaged Europe, and to this day the effects of those religious conflicts are felt culturally and politically. In the last century, the entire world was caught up in two terrible wars, born of, and sustained by, nationalistic striving. In very recent years, millions of people have been slaughtered in the course of tribal disputes in Rwanda, Darfur, and the Balkans. And it seems as though, from time immemorial, the Middle East has been torn by pitiless struggles between hostile groups. In Christ Jesus, the baby of Bethlehem, we see a way past these particularizing obsessions. Union with the God-Man, participation in the universal redemption wrought in him, strikes spiritually attentive people as infinitely more important than defending the prerogatives of any nation-state, any culture, any tribe.

This motif of universality, hinted in the Magi narrative, occurs regularly throughout the Gospels. Jesus is so amazed at the uncomplicated faith of the Roman centurion, whose servant the Lord has promised to heal, that he cries out: "Not in all of Israel have I encountered faith such as this." When the Syro-Phoenecian woman demonstrates the tenacity of her trust, Jesus praises and rewards. Toward the end of John's Gospel, Philip (himself bearing a Greek name) tells Jesus that Greek-speaking visitors have arrived to converse with him. In a gesture of unintended evangelism, Pontius Pilate places over the cross of Jesus a sign declaring him to be the king of Jews, and he is careful to write the message out in Hebrew, Latin, and Greek, assuring that it would go out to all the world. And at the death of Jesus, we are told, the curtain in the temple was torn in two from top to bottom, thereby revealing to the world the secret of the holy of holies: the spiritual secret the Jews had preserved so carefully over the centuries is now available to everyone. In all of these ways, the transnationalism of Jesus, anticipated in the story of the Magi, is brought into sharper relief.

What emerged from the Paschal Mystery, moreover, was not an institution or a nation-state, nor even a new religion, but rather a mystical body, an international, transcultural organism, whose ultimate purpose is the Christification of the world. In this mystical body, in Christ, there is indeed no Jew or Greek, for in that body,

67

national, racial, and ethnic differences have been situated within a higher context, subordinated to a more inclusive end. God knows that throughout the history of that body, churchmen have been personally compromised by nationalism and sectarianism and that the institution of the church has at times fallen prey to the worst kinds of temptations toward violence. But at its best, and according to its deepest identity, it has always embodied this universalizing ideal.

During the Middle Ages, in the time of Christendom, the internationalism of the church was concretely on display. Thomas Aquinas, an Italian, could learn his Aristotle from an Irish monk, be trained in theology by a German friar, and find his academic home at a French university. And he would die while traveling to an ecclesial council at Lyon, designed to solve the problem of the East-West divide within Christianity. More than a century before the time of Aquinas, St. Anselm, born in the north of Italy, could become a monk and eventually abbot at a Norman monastery before ending his life as the archbishop of Canterbury in England — a career trajectory virtually unimaginable today. Lord Kenneth Clark, the great British art historian, commented that internationalism holds sway precisely in regard to those things we consider most important — which is why, today, science and business are effortlessly international and why, in the Middle Ages, religion was so.

One of the signal accomplishments of John Paul II was the series of World Youth Days he sponsored throughout his papacy. John Paul gathered young people from all across the globe in Compostela, Paris, Denver, Toronto, Manila, and Rome. He wanted them to celebrate their ethnicity and nationality, to be sure, but he desired that, despite their enormous diversity, they see the unity they enjoyed through the church. He wanted them to appreciate that they were part of an organism whose contours stretched beyond national boundaries and cultural divides. He wanted them to know that their citizenship in the church was more basic and important than their citizenship in their respective nation-states. (Many viewed the arrival of millions of young people to pay tribute to, and pray for, John Paul at his funeral Mass as a rather striking sign of his success.)

In doing this, John Paul stood in a very long tradition of Christian internationalism, stretching back through the twenty centuries of the church's life, to the time of Peter and Paul, to the cross from which the universal kingship of Christ was proclaimed, all the way to the child of Bethlehem, visited by three kings from distant lands. The very catholicity of Christ and his mystical body is a light to the riven world.

THE GOOD SAMARITAN
A Portrait of Christ
Luke 10:29–37

T HE STORY OF the Good Samaritan is probably the best known of Jesus' parables. And the moral lesson contained in this narrative — that one should reach out to the suffering person, no matter what social, racial, or religious animosities might exist between helper and helped — is perennially pertinent. But something that both the fathers of the church and the Protestant theologian Karl Barth have taught me is that all things in the New Testament — stories, moral exhortations, letters, and parables — are finally descriptions of Jesus, portraits, however indirect, of the Lord. In one of the great painted windows of Chartres Cathedral, there is depicted the intertwining of two biblical stories: the account of the fall of the human race and the parable of the Good Samaritan. This artistic juxtaposition reflects a connection that was made from earliest centuries of the church between the figure of the Good Samaritan and Jesus the savior. It is this provocative symbolic suggestion that I should like to explore.

Jesus' story begins as follows: "There was a man going down from Jerusalem to Jericho." Jerusalem is a symbol of heaven, Mt. Zion — the place where, as Isaiah predicted, all of the tribes of the Lord will go up. Read mystically, therefore, Jerusalem signals the state of friendship with God. And as any attentive reader of the Hebrew Scriptures would know, Jericho evokes the city of sin, for it was the place that the invading Israelites had to conquer as they moved into the Promised Land. The journey from Jerusalem to Jericho is thus a symbol of the fall, the downward progression of the human race from unity with God to alienation from him. As the parable unfolds, we hear that "the man fell in with robbers." This is a realistic detail, since that road was notorious in Jesus' time as a haunt of bandits, but there is also a symbolic resonance. Sin effectively robs us of friendship with God and thereby corrupts all that is good in us. When we know the world apart from God, we know it less truly and less well; when our wills function in alienation from God, they do so errantly and awkwardly; when our passions are divorced from God, they become disordered and fall into a kind of civil war. Now all of this debilitation robs

71

us of our dignity and corrodes the image of God according to which we were created. Those who have been the victims of a robbery often say that the worst part of the experience is the humiliation of it — and this same dynamic holds when the robbery is a spiritual one. Next we hear that "they stripped him, and then went off, leaving him half-dead." What a perfect description of sin! In its wake, we are alive, but barely, for the divine life in us has been compromised; we are like the Gerasene demoniac, alive but wandering among the tombs, half-dead.

The parable is a tightly scripted drama, and now we turn to act two. "A priest happened to be going down the same road; he saw him, but continued on. Likewise there was a Levite who came the same way; he saw him and went on." To be sure, this is a sharp criticism of our unwillingness to take care of people in need; there is certainly a moral lesson to be learned here. If we pursue our Christological reading, however, unexpected dimensions open up. The priest and the Levite symbolize official religion, pious practice, the works of the law — all of the efforts of Israelite religion to affect salvation. These disciplines are not, of course, bad in themselves, but in accord with Paul's constant observation, they are, in their fallen state, unable to save us. Walking from Jerusalem to Jericho, the two pious figures stand for religion that has itself been compromised by sin, devolving into an exercise in self-justification. Those who have been beaten up and left half-dead by sin should, therefore, not expect aid from that particular quarter.

Now comes the hinge upon which the parable turns: "But a Samaritan who was journeying along came on him and was moved to pity at the sight." Samaritans were half-breeds, the descendants of those Jews who remained behind at the time of the exile and allowed themselves to mix sexually and culturally with non-Jewish tribes. Their very presence, therefore, was repulsive to Jews of pure blood. Jesus was a Jew, but he mingled so prodigally with sinners, outsiders, the morally suspect that he became, in the course of his public ministry, an object of suspicion. Finally, at the close of his life, all of polite society turned away from him. He *is*, therefore, the Samaritan. What does this despised traveler do? "He approached him and dressed his wounds, pouring in oil and wine as a means to heal." In his letter to the Philippians, Paul says of Jesus, "Though he was in the form of God, Jesus did not deem equality with God a thing to be grasped at, but rather emptied himself, taking the form of a slave." The Son of God was not pleased to remain in his heaven, but rather took to himself a human nature by which he could enter as radically as possible into the condition of the fallen human race. He *approached* us, even in our repugnant state, stooping down in order to raise us up.

73

What is more, he healed us. One of the earliest titles given to Jesus is *Soter* (healer, in the Greek), rendered in Latin as *salvator* (bearer of the *salus,* the salve, the healing balm). Christ is the great healer. And how does he heal? Once more the symbolism of the parable is striking: he pours in oil and wine. The alert Christian reader immediately interprets these as evocative of the sacraments of baptism, confirmation, and orders (all of which involve anointing) and Eucharist (wine consecrated to be the blood of Jesus). The author of the Gospel of John makes much the same sacramental point when he tells us that from the pierced side of Jesus there flowed water (baptism) and blood (the Eucharist).

We then hear that "he hoisted him on his own beast and brought him to an inn, where he cared for him." In his dying, Jesus took upon himself the sins of the world; in Paul's even more dramatic language, he became sin on the cross, bearing in his own body the suffering of the human race — hoisting us, as it were, upon himself. And then he brought us to the church, a place of rest and recuperation, where he continues, through the word, sacraments, and the community itself, to care for us. The narrative closes with a sharp symbolic detail: "The next day, he took out two silver pieces and gave them to the innkeeper and said, 'Take care of him; and when I come back, I will repay you whatever you spend.'" A word frequently used to describe what Jesus accomplished in his dying and rising is "redemption," from the Latin *redemere,* which means simply "to buy back." Christ Jesus paid the price for sin; he redressed the imbalance that it caused; he reestablished justice in God's cosmos. And thus we live as debtors no longer; we've been paid for.

We recall that the telling of this parable was prompted by the question of a man who "wished to justify himself" and asked, "who is my neighbor?" Jesus turns the table on him by asking, at the close of his narrative, "Which of these three was neighbor to the man who fell in with the robbers?" When the answer comes, "the one who treated him with compassion," Jesus says, with devastating simplicity: "Go and do the same." Having been saved by Christ, who became a neighbor to us, we must spend our lives becoming neighbor to those in need, scouting the road for those who have been brutalized by sin, and then endeavoring to pour in the wine and the oil. Having read this story as an icon of Jesus, we must become what we have seen.

THE MYSTERY OF LIGHT
Matthew 17:1–8

F REQUENTLY IN THE COURSE of the liturgical year the church invites us to reflect on the strange story of the Transfiguration of the Lord. In all three of the synoptic Gospels we hear that Jesus went up a high mountain — that place of contact with God — and was there transfigured in the presence of three of his disciples. "His face," Matthew tells us, "became as dazzling as the sun and his clothes as radiant as light." This luminous transformation of Jesus has bedazzled mystics and inspired artists and poets throughout the Christian centuries. There is a terrific depiction of the scene in one of the stained-glass windows on the façade of Chartres Cathedral. When, at the close of the day, the setting sun shines directly on this particular window, the figure of Jesus does indeed become incandescent, glowing like a jewel.

What does this event mean, and why does the church ask us to mediate upon it so regularly? Thomas Aquinas devotes an entire question in the third part of the *Summa theologiae* to a consideration of the Transfiguration, and his treatment sums up much of the wisdom of the church fathers on this matter. So let us attend with some care to his interpretation. Aquinas says that it was fitting for Christ to be manifested in his glory to his select apostles, because those who walk an arduous path need a clear sense of the goal of their journey. The arduous path that Thomas speaks of is this life, with all of its attendant sufferings, failures, setbacks, disappointments, anxieties, and injustices. Beset by all of this negativity, a pilgrim on life's way can easily succumb to despair unless he is granted a glimpse of the glory that comes at the end of his striving. And this is why, Aquinas argues, Jesus, while on his way to the cross, for a brief moment allows the light to shine through him. This is why he permits the end of the journey to appear, however fleetingly, in the midst of the journey. Though we live and move within the confines of this world of space and time, we are not meant, finally, for this dimensional system; we are summoned to life on high with God, in a transformed state of existence. The Transfiguration, therefore, awakens our sense of wonder and steels our courage to face the darkness here below.

Next Aquinas inquires more precisely after the light (*claritas*, in his Latin) that is said to have shone from the face and figure of Christ. A resurrected body, Thomas says, has four distinctive qualities: impassibility (it is beyond suffering), agility (it can move freely), subtlety (it is not obstructed by material obstacles), and clarity (it shines). Why have people, through history and across cultures, associated holiness with light? Why are saints, in our tradition, pictured with luminous haloes around their heads? Why have some people, even in our own time, seen a sort of glow emanating from particularly spiritual figures such as Mother Teresa or Padre Pio? One reason, Thomas suggests, is that light is the quality by which we see. Holy people provide a sort of interpretive grid to our experience; their form of life turns on the light that allows us to perceive the truth of things more clearly. But the most fundamental reason that we associate holiness with light is that light is beautiful and sanctity is beautiful above all. Aquinas says that Jesus, at the Transfiguration, began to shine with the radiance of heaven so as to entrance us with the prospect of our own beautiful transfiguration.

After considering Jesus himself, Thomas turns to the "witnesses" of the event. Two are figures from Israelite history (Moses and Elijah), and three are contemporaries of Jesus (Peter, James, and John). This juxtaposition of past and present is important, Aquinas maintains, because the salvation won by Christ properly transcends time, drawing into its power those who came before and those who would come after. Moses and Elijah symbolize the past; the apostles, who would carry the Gospel to the world, signify the future. All dimensions of time are drawn toward the magnetic point of the cross and resurrection. This same collapsing of the distinctions between the modalities of time occurs at the Mass, when the past is brought to the present and the present is carried to the eschatological fulfillment at the end of time. Moses, Elijah, Peter, James, and John are therefore a kind of prototype of the eucharistic community.

But we can also speak of each of these characters more specifically. Moses, of course, stands for the Law, the Torah. Jesus is consistently presented in the Gospels as the fulfillment of the Torah and as the new Moses. Thus, even as a child, he is, like Moses, hunted down; and when he gives the Sermon on the Mount, he appears as the Mosaic lawgiver par excellence. The Gospels imply that what was presented to Moses on tablets of stone has been offered perfectly through Jesus. The order and logic of God — visible truly but inadequately through the commands, prohibitions, and practices of the Old Law — are now fully, personally, and compellingly present in Jesus himself. This is why he can say, "I have come not to abolish the law but to fulfill it." He is not so much a better lawgiver than Moses as he is the Law made flesh. The correlation between these two revelations of the divine order is elegantly expressed in the conversation between Moses and Jesus.

And Elijah stands for prophecy, for he was generally perceived as the greatest of the prophets. Elijah, Elisha, Amos, Hosea, Isaiah, Jeremiah, Ezekiel, Daniel, and all of their prophetic confreres spoke the truth about God to varying degrees of intensity and in relation to various circumstances. But Jesus is not simply one more speaker of divine truth, not merely the greatest of the prophets: he *is* the divine Word, he is in person and in its entirety what all the prophets witnessed to from the outside and in fragmentary ways. It is this analogical relationship between Truth and truth-telling that is on display in the conversation between Jesus and Elijah. Both Moses and Elijah evanesce in the presence of Jesus, finding themselves by losing themselves, saying with John the Baptist, "He must increase and we must decrease."

Finally, Thomas turns to the contemporary witnesses. Why is Peter there? Because, says Aquinas, he loved the Lord the most. After the resurrection, Jesus asks Peter, "Simon, do you love me more than these?" When he receives a positive answer, he commands Peter to feed his sheep. Why is John there? Because he is the one whom the Lord loved the most. We know that throughout the Gospel that bears his name, John is referred to indirectly as "the disciple whom Jesus loved." What is implied here is something that the theologian Hans Urs von Balthasar intuited — that those who understand Jesus are those who enter into a relationship of love with him. "Getting" him is not so much a matter of clarity of mind as intensity of affection. Conversely, those who don't understand him — the Pharisees, the rich young man, Judas, and Pilate come readily to mind — are those who refuse his friendship. Therefore, Peter and John saw the Transfiguration, not because they were the cleverest or most powerful among the apostles, but because they had fallen in love with the Lord.

Now why was James permitted to see the vision? Because, Thomas says, James was the first of Jesus' intimate followers to prove the intensity of his love for Christ by giving his life: he would become the first martyr among the apostles. Love is desiring the good of the other as other. Therefore, there is no greater test of love than one's willingness to die for the object of one's love. This is the test that James would endure; and this is why James was privileged to see.

The meaning of the Old Testament revelation, the goal of the spiritual journey, the nature of the resurrected life, the condition for the possibility of seeing the Lord — all of it is illumined in the strange light of the Transfiguration.

Part Three

Life in the Spirit

THE HYMN TO LOVE

1 Corinthians 13:1–13

I N THE THIRTEENTH CHAPTER of Paul's first letter to
the Corinthians, we find one of the most compelling
and beautiful texts in the Sacred Scriptures, the so-called
"hymn to love." Love, we hear, is the greatest and most
enduring of the theological virtues (those "three things
that last"), surpassing in importance both hope and faith.
"If you have faith strong enough to move mountains, but
have not love, you are nothing." To realize the significance of that particular ranking, all we have to do is
consult Paul's letter to the Romans, where the salvific
centrality of faith is explained so rapturously and so un-
ambiguously. What is more, love outstrips any of the
impressive manifestations of the spirit that appeared in
the Pauline communities: "If I speak with the tongues of
mortals and angels, but do not have love, I am a noisy
gong or a clanging cymbal." Finally, love is greater than
even the most morally heroic act: "If I give away all

my possessions and if I hand over my body so that I may boast, but do not have love, I gain nothing." Paul intuited something that has remained central to the Christian tradition for two thousand years: since love *is* the divine life, to live in love is to participate in God. Whereas faith opens the door to God and hope orders us to God as our final end, love is what God *is*. And this is precisely why Paul tells us that faith and hope will fade away in heaven, whereas love will not. Immersed in the divine being, we will need neither faith (for we will see clearly) nor hope (for we will have the good that we want), but we will need love, for love is what it means to be immersed in this way.

But what precisely is love? We have a tendency, especially in our rather romantic culture, to identify it with a feeling or a sentiment. But authentic love, in the biblical sense, is only marginally related to emotions. To love is to will the good of the other as other, really to want what is advantageous to another person and to act concretely on that desire. This is to be distinguished then from all forms of indirect egotism: doing something good for others so that they might return the favor. Love involves an ecstatic leap outside the narrow confines of one's own preoccupations and needs — which explains why real love is such a rare phenomenon. It also explains why enemy love is the fullest test of love. When you desire the good of someone who is not the least bit likely to return the favor, you know that your desire is pure, unadulterated by egotism.

With this fundamental clarification in mind, we can more deeply appreciate the nuanced analysis that Paul gives us in the second part of the hymn to love. The Apostle tells us first that "love is patient; love is kind." When you want the good of the other and not your own good, you are willing to wait. A sure sign that one is being merely superficially benevolent is a lack of patience in the face of the other's recalcitrance. "I've done so much for him, and he doesn't even acknowledge my presence," imperfect lovers find themselves saying. But true lovers wait, continuing to forgive, even when no reciprocal forgiveness is forthcoming, continuing to be kind, even when no answering kindness ensues. Real love is patient because it doesn't calculate or measure or weigh according to the demands of strict justice; rather, in the manner of a parent who loves her child in season and out, it watches the other in hope.

Next, Paul tells us that "love is not envious." When you really desire the good of the other, you don't resent that person's success or joy. The American novelist Gore Vidal beautifully summed up the attitude of jealousy in this admission: "When a friend of mine succeeds, something in me dies." Vidal made his observation more pointed, commenting that he burned with jealousy at the successes of the celebrated playwright Tennessee Williams, precisely because Williams was so close to him personally. When I first came across that quotation, I experienced, unpleasantly enough, a shock of recognition. How often, I mused, have I remained indifferent to the triumphs of strangers, while silently but deeply resenting the achievements of friends. There seems to be a perverse proportionality at work in the dynamics of jealousy: the more closely related the person, the deeper the envy she awakens. But authentic love *wants* the good of the other and therefore delights in the joys and attainments of others. The practitioner of love realizes a truth taught consistently throughout the Bible — that the being of the lover increases precisely through the good of the beloved, since both are, at the depths of their being, one.

As the hymn to love unfolds, we hear that love "does not put on airs; it is not snobbish." Our economic, political, and social lives are, it is sad to say, predicated to a large degree on the very opposite impulse. From the time we are children, we instinctively seek higher positions and more impressive titles that we might establish our superiority over others. We spend much of our lives desperately jockeying for every advantage, impressing whom we can and destroying whom we must; for we realize that if we don't act aggressively, we will be supplanted. In this terrible zero-sum game, if you are noticed and celebrated, I am forgotten, and if you advance, I am forced to retreat. Though most of the players in this tournament are far too deft to let it show publicly, they are engaged continually in a cutthroat competition, destroying their opponents even as they smile at them over cocktails. But love *wants* the good of the other; it *wants* the other to succeed and to be noticed. Therefore, it is, as Paul says, self-effacing, self-forgetting, willing to let the other shine and bear the privileged title — willing, in the manner of John the Baptist, to decrease while someone else increases.

Next we hear that love is "not prone to anger, nor does it brood over injuries." In Dante's *Divine Comedy,* the angry are punished on Mt. Purgatory by being made to choke on thick smoke. The punishments in Dante are never arbitrary, always relating to the sin they address. In this case, the angry are compelled to experience the effects of anger: its manner of clouding the vision and strangling coherent speech. When we read the world through the cloud of our own anger, we get a deeply distorted picture, and when we attempt to speak while choking on our own bitterness, our speech is sputtering and ineffectual. Licking our wounds, reminding ourselves how deeply we've been hurt, nursing decades-old grudges, we shrink into a very small space, and our communication with others becomes, at best, garbled, distorted. But to will the good of the other as other — to love — is to break out of this prison. When we love, we let go of our brooding self-regard and our ultimately self-destructive patterns of resentment.

Paul then says that love "does not rejoice in what is wrong, but rejoices with the truth." If we turn around Gore Vidal's observation, we come up with what the Germans call *Schadenfreude,* taking pleasure in another's misfortune. Obviously, this tendency to rejoice in the pain of the other is the precise opposite of love, but how gleefully most of us sinners indulge in it. So thrilled are we at the failure or embarrassment of someone else that we become evangelists of it, announcing it to anyone willing to listen. If we do a serious examination of conscience, most of us would discover that much of our day is spent in this spiritually debilitating exercise. Real love, Paul is telling us, finds no joy in another's pain and is loath to serve it up, through gossip, to an eager audience. Rather, love finds joy in the truth of things, and the truth is that we are all connected by the deepest metaphysical bonds. And therefore, mocking another or intensifying his pain by reveling in it is repugnant to love.

Paul concludes his great hymn by reminding us that knowledge will fail, the speaking in tongues will cease, prophecies will die away, but that love never dies. We will take none of our earthly titles, degrees, or "religious" achievements with us to heaven, but we will indeed carry there the quality of our love. Therefore, order your life according to this great and abiding act.

THE LAW OF THE GIFT

Genesis 22:1–14

THE MOST TERRIFYING STORY in the Old Testament is told in the twenty-second chapter of the book of Genesis. Precisely because of its fearsomeness, this narrative compels us to come to grips with some of the most fundamental truths concerning ourselves and our faith. It unfolds with the brevity and understatement typical of the Bible. God tells Abraham that he wants him to sacrifice his only son, the child of his old age and the sole bearer of his family name. Obedient, Abraham sets out to do so, journeying over the course of three days to the mountain of sacrifice. At the last moment, as he is raising the knife to dispatch the son he loves, Abraham is stopped by an angel of God.

The rabbis and midrashic commentators of the Jewish tradition especially loved this story of the Aqedah (the binding), and their observations and interpretations have enormously enhanced our appreciation of it. Isaac, they remind us, was everything to his father. Practically from the moment that he commenced his relationship with Abraham, God had told the patriarch that he would become the progenitor of a great nation — indeed, that his descendants would be more numerous than the stars in the heavens or the sands on the shore of the sea. As he grew older and this promise seemed increasingly unlikely, Abraham continued to believe. When he was a very old man, Abraham was visited by three mysterious travelers who, having eaten the meal he had prepared for them, made an extraordinary prediction: upon their return at the same time the following year, Abraham's wife, Sara, impossibly past the age of child-bearing, would be the mother of a son. So ludicrous did this seem that Sara, overhearing their words, laughed out loud. But Sara did conceive, and Isaac, the promised one, the bearer of the covenant, was born before the year was out. To call Isaac the apple of his father's eye or the treasure of his heart would be hopeless understatement.

But then God wants him to offer this son as a burnt offering (holocaust). The Bible does not speak of Abraham's utter confusion and consternation at this request, but the commentaries do. His suffering was not only emotional but, if I can put it this way, theological. How could the same God who made a binding oath, and who fulfilled it against all odds, now fall into contradiction with himself by demanding the death of the very son through whom he had promised Abraham innumerable descendants? It must have seemed like mockery of the cruelest sort. The midrashic tradition elaborates upon the terrible journey that Abraham makes with Isaac to Mt. Moriah. As they walked, talked, and camped over the three days, Isaac, like most children of twelve, must have been excited to be on an adventure with his father and must have inquired frequently about the purpose of their trip. How devastating beyond description this must have been to his father. When they came to the mountain, Abraham placed the wood of sacrifice on his son's narrow shoulders, and together they ascended. The most poignant and awful moment was undoubtedly when Isaac observed that there was fuel for the fire but no lamb for the sacrifice. Heartbroken, Abraham could muster only, "God will provide." Finally, there comes the staying of the hand that bore the knife, and the assurance of reward for the intensity of faith displayed.

If you don't feel some dark anguish upon hearing this story, you haven't been paying attention; if there isn't some anger welling up in you, you haven't grasped the disturbing core of the narrative. The philosopher Søren Kierkegaard wrote one of his best-known books, *Fear and Trembling,* in order to demonstrate that the "meaning" of the Aqedah is other than anything that philosophy, ethics, or conventional religion could possibly explicate. Kierkegaard could make articulate speech about any philosopher or hero, but in the presence of Abraham he was compelled into a sort of puzzled but reverential silence, for Abraham, in sacrificing his son, was actively willing the impossible, something the mind can't contain. Until we have experienced something of this intellectual vertigo, we haven't allowed the story to grasp us adequately.

This terrifying narrative is one of the most vivid displays of a paradoxical principle that can be found from beginning to end of the Bible, namely, the law of the gift. This spiritual maxim can be stated simply: your being increases and is enhanced in the measure that you give it away. And its corollary can be expressed with equal simplicity: your being decreases to the point of annihilation in the measure that you cling to it. The tale of the widow of Zarephath in the first book of Kings beautifully exemplifies the adage. The prophet Elijah asks the old woman for something to eat, and she informs him, matter-of-factly, that she has enough food to prepare one last meal for her and her son before they die. Upon hearing this rather desperate bit of news, Elijah asks her to make him a cake! But she agrees to his request and discovers that her oil and flour are replenished miraculously for the next year. We find the same idea in the Gospel account of the multiplication of the loaves and fishes. When a boy gives Jesus the little that he has, his gift is elevated and multiplied so as to feed five thousand people. And in the parable of the prodigal son, the corollary principle is made manifest. When the younger son grasps for his own what his father wants to give him as a gift, he loses what he has, wandering off into a "far country" of famine and humiliation.

What is Abraham willing to give away? That which he loves the most, the son of his old age, the child of promise. And the result is the increase of his being. At the heart of *Fear and Trembling* is Kierkegaard's analysis of faith as a "passion for the impossible," for Abraham was willing to sacrifice his son, even as he was convinced of the seemingly impossible idea that he would receive his son back. This is, of course, nonsense according to ordinary logic, but it is right according to the logic of the gift. We all must identify that which we love the most and then make of it an offering to God, and we will receive it back multiplied thirty-, sixty-, or a hundred-fold.

When the first Christians looked back at this archetypal narrative from their Jewish tradition, they discerned a remarkable resonance with the story of the sacrificial death of Jesus. At the Transfiguration, the disciples heard God speak: "A voice came from the cloud saying, 'This is my beloved son; listen to him.'" Just as Isaac was the cherished child of Abraham, Jesus, they learned, is the cherished son of God the Father. And after the mountaintop experience, Jesus told Peter, James, and John not to tell of what they had seen until after the Son of Man had risen from the dead, that is, until the paschal mystery of the cross and resurrection had unfolded. They are being compelled to see that the dynamic between the divine Father and the divine Son is one of giver and gift, of sacrificer and sacrificed, precisely in the manner of Abraham and Isaac. On Calvary, God the Father lays the wood of the cross on the shoulders of his Son and leads him up a hill where he will allow him to be sacrificed. The anguish Abraham felt as he brought Isaac to Mt. Moriah is a faint anticipation of the anguish God the Father feels as he hands his only-begotten Son over to the executioners. Like Abraham, the heavenly Father was willing to give away what was dearest to him, and the result, in accordance with the deep magic of the law of the gift, was an increase in being. Because of this self-gift on the part of the Father and this obedience on the part of the Son, the divine life became available to the whole sinful world. What was given came back as a gift, enhanced and multiplied.

Do you want joy and fullness of life? Then you must find a way to make of your life a gift, even if that means giving away what you cherish the most. Is this possible? According to the conventional logic of the world, no — it's impossible and ridiculous; but according to the logic of the gift, which is congruent with the deepest ground of reality, with the very being of God, decidedly yes.

THE AMBITIOUS HEART
Mark 10:35–45

THERE IS A SCENE in the tenth chapter of Mark's Gospel of special spiritual importance precisely for the way it tells us how *not* to approach Jesus. Up to the Lord come John and James, the sons of Zebedee, and they make a demand: "Teacher, we want you to do for us whatever we ask of you." Jesus is not one religious teacher among many — indeed, not one human being among many. Rather, he is the very Logos of God in the flesh, the incarnation of the eternal Word. As such, he can never be positioned by something or someone outside of himself; he can never be situated in a higher context or examined in light of analytical principles independent of him. Instead, he positions everything and everybody else; he asks the questions, and he does the analyzing. Thus James and John are on extremely shaky ground when they make their brash demand. In fact, they are in a spiritual space similar to that inhabited by

99

Martha when she said to Jesus, "Tell my sister to help me." As the church fathers commented in connection with that command of Martha: "You know that all is not well with you when you start telling God what to do!"

Nevertheless, Jesus patiently inquires what it is that they want from him. The answer comes: "Grant that in your glory we may sit, one at your right and the other at your left." There is the unadulterated voice of ambition, one of the most powerful motivators in the human experience. Some people could care less about money, power, or pleasure, but they are passionately interested in glory — that is to say, the aggrandizing of the ego. James and John, desiring to be second and third when Jesus assumes his throne as the warrior king of Israel, are rather clearly of this type. To be fair to them, they are doing what ambitious young men at the beginning of their careers (I always imagine them as youthful) have perennially done. They are cannily aligning themselves to a powerful figure on the rise, so that they can bask in his reflected glory when he "arrives." A religiously and politically alert Israelite of the time could certainly be expected to see in Jesus a likely candidate for Davidic Messiah, the one who, if the prophets are right, would rule Israel and, eventually, all the nations of the world.

Having heard them, Jesus turns the tables on them: "You do not know what you are asking." He will indeed be a king, and he will indeed rule Israel, but his crown will be made of thorns, and his throne will be a Roman instrument of torture. He will indeed come into his glory, but his glory will be that of a love unto death. In the Gospel of John, Jesus says, "When the Son of Man is raised up, he will draw all people to himself." But the raising up in question has nothing to do with worldly honor, and the drawing has nothing to do with crude ambition. Rather, he will be raised up on his cross, and to that terrible height he will call all people, including James and John.

As he continues his conversation with his young disciples, Jesus asks, "Can you drink the cup that I drink or be baptized with the baptism with which I am baptized?" What the question implies is that authentic glory is inextricably bound to drinking the cup of suffering and to being, out of love, submerged (baptized) under the waters of death. And so one must be careful what one asks for.

In his great autobiographical prayer, the *Confessions*, St. Augustine tells of an encounter he had on the streets of Milan. He was on his way to an oration by the emperor of Rome, which Augustine himself, in his capacity as imperial rhetorician, had composed. He was inordinately proud of his achievement, appreciating it as the fulfillment of a lifelong dream. We recall that Augustine had been born in the tiny North African town of Tagaste, a village of which the sophisticated citizens of Rome, Athens, and Ravenna had not the slightest inkling. The young, gifted man was sent to Carthage, the most important city in his region. There he studied grammar, logic, and rhetoric, becoming in time an extremely fine Latin stylist and a clever philosopher. What the young Augustine wanted above all was to make it at the imperial court, to be a writer for the most influential men in the world. In accord with that ambition and through the help of friends, he landed a position in Rome as a professor of rhetoric, and eventually he was invited to Milan, where the emperor was then resident, to be an imperial speechwriter. Therefore, as he was being carried on his litter that day to hear his own literary creation coming from the lips of the emperor, Augustine sensed that, at long last, he had arrived.

Then came the encounter that changed his life. He spotted a pathetic figure, a man so drunk he could barely stand up, who was muttering incoherently to himself and making obscene gestures. We've all run into such characters on the streets of our major cities, and when we do, we usually turn away in embarrassment or cluck our tongues in disapproval. Such was Augustine's reaction. But then an insight came to him in a flash: "You are no different than this man!" The drunken man was so addicted to alcohol that his drinking had rendered him less than human. But Augustine was addicted to honor and glory, so ambitious for worldly fame that his every thought, word, and action was devoted to this end. He had, he realized, surrendered his life to "getting ahead" just as much as this sad figure had surrendered his life to alcohol. And this capitulation had indeed made him less than human. But then came an even more terrible insight: he, the great Augustine, rhetorician to the emperor, was in fact in worse shape than the pathetic street person. For the drunken man would eventually sober up and perhaps regret his excessive drinking, but Augustine had been drunk on ambition for years and showed neither the slightest sign of sobering up nor, until that moment, the slightest regret at his past behavior. There is a tight connection between this encounter on the streets of Milan and the lines found near the very beginning of the *Confessions:* "Lord, you have made us for yourself, and therefore our hearts are restless until they rest in thee." Both alcohol and ambition are pathetically inadequate correlates to the deepest longing of the heart. Though his disciples had approached him in precisely the wrong way, Jesus had patiently attended to the request of James and John and had tried, in various ways, to clarify and redirect their request. At the close of this passage, his final answer comes: "But to sit at my right or at my left is not mine to give but it is for those for whom it has been prepared." The Father has prepared the place for one who will be situated to Jesus' right when the Son of Man comes into his glory, for one who will reign with him. On Good Friday afternoon, the good thief turned to the crucified Jesus and made a request that was not altogether different from that of James and John. "Jesus, remember me when you come into your kingdom." And to him Jesus responded, "Truly, I tell you, this day you will be with me in Paradise." This crucified criminal was indeed in the very place that James and John, in their naïve ambition, coveted. The one who was drinking the same cup of suffering as Jesus was privileged to reign with him. Let there be no limit to your ambition, as long as it leads you to that place alongside of the crucified Christ.

THE SEVEN GIFTS
OF THE HOLY SPIRIT
Isaiah 11:1–3

I N THE ELEVENTH CHAPTER of the book of the prophet
Isaiah, we find a striking description of the Messiah
who is to come. We hear that a shoot shall sprout from
the stump of Jesse and that "from his roots a bud shall
blossom." In his typically lyrical and symbolic language,
Isaiah is asserting that the Messianic ruler will be, not the
scion of a royal dynasty, but a descendant of Jesse and
David, shepherds of Bethlehem. One of the stained-glass
windows on the western façade of Chartres Cathedral
beautifully depicts this prophecy. It shows a great plant
rising up out of the loins of a sleeping Jesse and on the
limbs of this tree are displayed, like leaves, all of his
descendants, the ancestors of the Messiah. Then Isaiah
tells us that the Davidic king will be endowed with an
array of gifts: "The spirit of the Lord will rest upon him:
a spirit of wisdom and understanding, a spirit of counsel

105

and of strength, a spirit of knowledge and fear of the Lord." In the Chartres window, the figure of the Messiah, on the top of Jesse's tree, is surrounded by seven doves, symbolic of these seven energies of the Spirit.

Because they are so tightly associated with Christ Jesus himself, the gifts of the Holy Spirit have been discussed, analyzed, and pondered throughout the great Christian tradition. Pope Gregory the Great, Augustine, and Thomas Aquinas are just a few of the prominent thinkers who have made a consideration of the gifts central to their presentation of the spiritual life. Therefore, all Christians can benefit from taking them seriously.

The first gift of the Spirit is *wisdom, sapientia* in Latin, *sophia* in Greek. Wisdom is a highly distinctive kind of knowing, one that Aquinas compares to the view from the mountaintop — that is to say, from the standpoint of God, the highest and all-embracing cause. Most of us look at our lives from the narrow perspective of our own desires, needs, and fears, and this leads to a distorting of vision, the tendency to miss the overarching and clarifying pattern. When Job complains to God about the gross injustice of his suffering, God takes him on an elaborate tour of the cosmos, introducing him to the rhythms of nature, the behavior patterns of obscure animals, and the constitution of the heavens. He draws him out of a self-regarding framework and toward the divine vantage point, where the entire causal nexus is visible. God thereby successfully places Job's experience of his own pain in a different context. One could say that the entire narrative of the book of Job culminates in the spiritual gift of wisdom — the capacity to see things, as far as it is possible for us, from the mountaintop.

The next two gifts — *understanding* and *knowledge* — are usually treated as a pair. Aquinas tells us that these refer to the capacity for insight into holy things and the truths of the faith. Most of us can move through our lives quite successfully and rarely ponder the deepest and most abiding realities. Though we might become expert in the theory and practice of banking, business, politics, or even sports, most of us never become theologically astute, never intensely interested in the Eucharist, the meaning of the cross, the whys and wherefores of the Incarnation, or the enigma of the Trinity.

I can imagine you smiling as you read this: who, you might wonder, besides priests and specialists in theology, would have the time, ability, or energy to think about such things? And yet this world, and all of its interests and diversions, is passing away. What we shall meditate upon for the whole of eternity are not the intricacies of finance or the strategies of corporate advancement; rather, we shall meditate upon the mysteries of the faith. The spiritual gifts of understanding and knowledge result in a participation, even now, in this mode of contemplation.

The next gift of the Holy Spirit is *counsel.* This is a practical power, the ability to make good moral and religious judgments. In the course of our careers, we make countless judgments regarding professional and personal matters: What sort of job should I take? Whom should I marry? What sort of house should I buy? But how often do we ever deliberate about questions such as "what kind of person do I want to be? What shape should my ethical life take? Am I growing in faith, hope, and love?" Brett Favre, the venerable quarterback for the Green Bay Packers, has an uncanny ability to read a defense and dissect a secondary, weaving his passes past defenders and into the arms of his receivers. He has, to put it more technically, practical prudence, a feel for the ever-shifting patterns of the team arrayed against him. The spiritual gift of counsel is practical prudence in regard to the complexities of journeying toward God. It is a feel for the game of becoming holy, a knack for answering the spiritual questions rightly. St. Therese of Lisieux's "little way" is born of the gift of counsel, for it is nothing other than a prudential instinct in regard to the will of the Holy Spirit: in every concrete situation, no matter how trivial, what is the loving thing to do?

Fortitude is the next spiritual gift. As everyone can attest, being good, in the context of a fallen, conflictual world, is a struggle. Very often we know what to do, but we cannot muster the capacity or the energy to do it. In the seventh chapter of his letter to the Romans, Paul gave classic expression to this truth when he said, "The good that I would do, I do not; and the evil that I would avoid, that I do." There are stumbling blocks — both internal and external — to moral rectitude, and these can be overcome only by strengthening the spiritual fiber, toughening the character. This empowerment is fortitude. Jesus himself exemplified this gift of the Spirit in the Garden of Gethsemane when he successfully resisted enormous internal pressures and overwhelming external threats in order to carry out his Father's will. Thomas More embodied it when, over the course of many years, he stared down the various menaces and enticements Henry VIII put before him in order to dissuade More from following his conscience. And Maximilian Kolbe showed that he had been endowed with it when he volunteered to take the place of a man condemned to death and endured weeks of an agonizing execution by starvation. Now these are extreme and dramatic examples. An ordinary person exhibits fortitude when he perdures in the faith despite the mocking of his colleagues, or when she does the right thing despite the fear of being ostracized. Like other forms of toughening, fortitude can and should be intensified through exercise.

The sixth gift of the Holy Spirit is *piety.* Unfortunately, "pious" is an unimpressive word in contemporary English — calling to mind fussy, superficial, and often hypocritical people whom our culture likes to satirize. But neither Isaiah nor the theologians of the great tradition have any of this in mind when they speak of piety. For them, this gift is an instinctual feel for what is owed to God. Now what we owe to God is everything, and therefore the pious person is deeply aware of her obligation to praise God and to worship him. This is why piety is the great virtue that undergirds the liturgy. Thomas Aquinas commented that we attend Mass as an act of justice, rendering to God the praise and thanksgiving that is his due on account of the gift of creation. How far this is from our contemporary sense of worshiping in order to evoke a spiritual experience.

The seventh and final gift of the Spirit is *fear of the Lord.* Aquinas says that there are two basic forms of fear: servile and filial. The first is the fear that a slave has in the presence of his master, or that an employee might have when confronted by his angry boss. It is trepidation at the prospect of punishment. But the second fear is that which a son might have before his beloved father.

It is not so much a fear of being punished as a deep regret that a precious relationship might be lost. It is this second type of fear that is a gift of the Holy Spirit, for it is the feeling that leads someone away from those attitudes and acts that might compromise his friendship with God, the relationship which is more important than anything else. When the Bible speaks — as it often does — of the "fear of the Lord," it implies this healthy concern that intimacy with God might never be lost.

Having briefly surveyed the seven gifts, the natural question arises: how does one come by them? They cannot be acquired in the manner of natural virtues through habituation and resolute effort. They are, after all, *gifts.* But since they flow from Jesus Christ, they come to those who establish an intimacy with Jesus in the church and the sacraments, especially the Eucharist. St. Augustine said that we pray in order to expand our wills to make them capacious enough to receive what God wants to give us. So perhaps the best thing that we can do in order to receive the seven gifts is, with expansiveness of heart, to ask for them.

A LIVING SACRIFICE
OF PRAISE
Romans 12:1–2

THE CLOSING CHAPTERS of Paul's letter to the Romans constitute one of the first moral theologies in the Christian tradition — the Apostle instructing the little Christian community at Rome how to live in accord with the spirit of Jesus. Though Martin Luther drove a wedge between faith and good works — and claimed Paul as his principle inspiration — there is little in the letter to the Romans to justify such a division. The same Paul who, in the opening chapters of Romans, spoke so passionately of justification through grace, spoke just as insistently of the ethical demand in the final section of that same letter.

I would like to focus on a line from the twelfth chapter of Romans that succinctly articulates the Christian approach to ethics in general; this one line has particular relevance to the matter of sexual morality. Paul says, "I urge you, brothers and sisters, by the mercies of God, to offer your bodies as a living sacrifice, holy and pleasing to God, your spiritual worship."

Paul was not a dualist. He did not believe, in the manner of Plato and his disciples, that spirit and matter belong to two utterly distinct metaphysical arenas. And he certainly didn't think that the purpose of the spiritual life is to facilitate the escape of the soul from the body. No, Paul was a Jew and, as such, he used the term "body" to designate the whole of the self: muscles, bones, and sexuality, but also mind and emotions. What he tells the Christians at Rome is that this entire self should be offered to God as a sacrifice. It's been said that if we traveled to the ancient world in a time machine, we would be most surprised by the prevalence of religious sacrifice in that milieu. In Paul's time, people would regularly slaughter animals and offer their flesh to God or the gods as a sign of love, thanksgiving, or propitiation. So Paul is suggesting that we should think about the moral life, not so much legalistically as liturgically, not primarily as the fulfilling of regulations but rather as the sending up of a prayer. The whole of our existence, from day to day, should be a sustained act of honoring God with our bodies.

An ancient person would bring to sacrifice a pure lamb, an unblemished dove, or the first fruits of the harvest — something expressive of the quality of his devotion and worthy of the god he was honoring. To bring to sacrifice a third-rate offering would be liturgically inappropriate — insulting to God and denigrating to the self. Thus Paul's exhortation implies a question: What is the quality of the body that we place as a living sacrifice on the altar of God? Is it a body that has performed works of hatred and violence, said hurtful things, reached out to attack, or walked away from the poor and needy? If so, it is hardly a fit vehicle for the proper worship of God.

Not long ago, I was at a friend's house and was surfing my way through his wide selection of cable channels, when I stumbled across MTV's program on spring break. Now, I don't think I'm remarkably prudish in matters sexual, but I have to confess that what I saw disturbed me. It wasn't so much the amount of flesh and explicit sexual behavior (though that was excessive enough); it was the attitude. It was clear that for the young people on that program, sex is purely recreational, something one does for entertainment. Sexual contact seemed to be in the same genre of harmless self-indulgent fun as drinking, smoking, or lying in the sun. My strong impression was that anyone suggesting a link between sex and committed love would have been promptly laughed off the stage.

Just a few weeks after my MTV experience, I read a book by the psychologist and physician Leonard Sax called *Why Gender Matters*. It's a fascinating study of the physical and psychological differences between the genders and how those should affect the way we think about the education of children. But what particularly caught my attention in Sax's book was the chapter on sexual behavior among young men and women. Sax observed that in the past twenty-five or thirty years there has been a remarkable shift in this area. Thirty years ago, most of those who engaged in extramarital sex still had some sense of a connection between personal commitment and physical expression: young people of that time would justify even their relatively irresponsible sex through some appeal to love. But now, Sax argues, young people increasingly engage in sex of the most casual and impersonal kind, and they do so with an attitude of indifference and impunity. In particular, the resistance that young women would have shown, just thirty years ago, has now disappeared, females having surrendered to the more impulsive sexuality of males. Sax comments that this casualness in regard to sex has led to myriad psychological problems in the young men and women who crowd his and his colleagues' offices for consultation. And he concludes that the solution is to place sexual contact within the context of loving, committed relationships.

Well, in saying so, he joins an impressive chorus of voices — Moses, Isaiah, Jeremiah, Ezekiel, and Paul, to name just a few — from the great biblical tradition.

Part of what it means to offer one's body as a living sacrifice of praise is to present one's sexuality to God as something pure, excellent, and unsullied, something like unto God himself. But God *is* love. Therefore, the sexuality that we place on the altar should be a vehicle and expression of love, a gift of self. When sex devolves into a crude means to self-gratification, it becomes a sacrifice unworthy of God and denigrating to the self. Don't think of God, by the way, as a prim, school-marmish moralist, making arbitrary demands upon us. God has no *need* of our sacrifices or our moral excellence, for God needs nothing at all. But God wants something — namely, our joy and our fullness of life — and this comes when we freely offer ourselves in love as a living sacrifice, for in that act, we become like God.

Paul concludes this section of his letter to the Romans with these words: "Do not conform yourselves to this age, but be transformed by the renewal of your mind." He was talking about the pagan culture of ancient Rome, so marked by self-indulgence and violence; but he could just as well have been speaking of our own culture, marred by secularism, subjectivism, and hedonism. How tragic if Christians simply mimic the self-regarding mores of the age in which they find themselves. How wonderful if they find a way to place their bodies as living sacrifices on the altar of God.

THE ANGELS
AND THE BEASTS
Mark 1:12–13

Medieval Christian scholars said that human beings are a kind of microcosm of the whole created order, since we bear within ourselves both the spiritual and the physical. Through our bodies we reach down to the lower elements and are one with the animals and minerals, but through our minds we commune with the upper realm of spirits and angels. We know instinctively how right this characterization is. On the one hand, we can explore the intricacies of mathematics and geometry; we can soar with Mozart and Shakespeare; we can design high-level computers and machines that move through the galaxy; we can enter into the depth and silence of mystical prayer, coming close to the angelic way of knowing. In all of these ways, we demonstrate the capaciousness of our souls. On the other hand, we are, whether we like it or not, animals. We need food and drink; we get too hot or too cold; we experience instincts and emotions that often get the better of our reason; we revel in the sheer pleasure of the senses and the thrill of being touched; we love to run and to exercise our muscles; we exult in the rough-and-tumble of very physical competition and play. This coming together of the spiritual and the material is our glory — since we combine, in a sense, the best of both worlds — but it is also our agony, the source of much of our sadness and conflict. A kind of metaphysical mongrel, we bring together in our very persons elements that are, often enough, at odds with one another. The spirit strains against the body (think of Michelangelo's "athletes" on the ceiling of the Sistine Chapel); and the body struggles against the spirit. Sometimes the mind commands, and matter refuses to obey, or matter makes demands that the mind cannot or will not accommodate.

One way to handle this problem is imperialist aggression, the dominance of spirit over body or body over spirit. Let us consider the first option. In so many philosophies and spiritualities — both East and West — we find a celebration of the transcendent spiritual capacity and a concomitant longing to escape from the drabness of materiality. Plato, for instance, thought that the entire philosophical life was but a preparation for the wonderful day when the soul — the angel-like spirit — would escape through death from the prison of the body.

119

One way to read Plato's *Republic* is as an intricately conceived training manual for prospective jailbreakers. Plotinus, an ardent disciple of Plato and one of the most influential philosophers of the late Roman period, was described by one of his followers as "never quite at home in his body" — and that was meant as a compliment. This dualist strain of thinking can be found in modernity as well. René Descartes, the founder of modern philosophy, starkly separated the body, which belongs to the realm of "extended things," from the mind, which is a "thinking thing," and this "angelism" conditions all of Descartes's program. At a more popular level, one can discover this preference of spirit over body in much of the New Age spiritualities of the present day. Just think of those sad members of a New Age cult who, not many years ago, committed suicide in the hopes of releasing their spirits from the "lower vehicles" of their earthly bodies.

But the imperialism comes from the opposite side as well, when the body seeks, as it were, to escape from the mind. Alongside of Platonism in the ancient world, there was the competing philosophy of hedonism, which put an exclusive stress on pleasure and the satisfaction of bodily desire. And up and down the centuries, this perspective has attracted many, from the Marquis de Sade to Hugh Hefner. On this reading, the "spiritual" dimension is something of an illusion — at best a more rarified form of bodily desire, and at worst a collection of inhibitions and complexes that ought to be repressed or deconstructed. For the hedonist, the human being is not qualitatively different from the other animals; rather, he is an especially clever beast, particularly adept at acquiring what his body craves. Think, in this context, of Sigmund Freud's insistence that the rational mind is not so much the tamer of the elemental desires as their servant. As is true in regard to political imperialism, which tends to stir up the resentment of the tyrannized party, so this psychological and spiritual imperialism leads, easily enough, to civil war within the person. When Plato and his disciples treat the body as a prison, the body reacts, often in psychologically destructive ways; and when the hedonists treat the mind as an epi-phenomenon of the body, the spirit rebels.

A third option does remain. A person can live alternately in the upper realm and the lower, keeping the one carefully sequestered from the other. One of the greatest theologians of the last century, a man of exquisite cultural and religious refinement, the author of a massive systematic theology and of deeply moving homilies, also frequented the red-light districts of the cities he visited and assembled an extensive collection of pornography. It was as though body and mind lived side by side in him, unintegrated and unrelated to one another. This sort of isolation of the elements of the self is no solution, for in the long run it leads to a radical bifurcation and disintegration of the personality.

Throughout the Bible, we find the claim — sometimes explicitly argued, other times implied — that these tensions between body and soul, these fundamental disintegrations, are symptoms of sin. In the Genesis account of creation, we hear that God made the whole of the cosmos, things seen and unseen, the spiritual as well as the physical. He made, as the crown of his efforts, a rational animal, capable of speech and divine communion, and he placed him within a garden of physical delights and surrounded him with all of his brother animals that fly through the air and creep and crawl upon the ground. But in the wake of the original sin, divisions begin to appear. Adam and Eve, who once were comfortable with their physicality, now seek to cover themselves, their bodies having become an object of shame. And nature, symbolized by the serpent, has now emerged as the enemy, the cunning tempter. This interpretation is confirmed in the story of the flood. We see that God protects from the waters (evocative of the power of sin) not only his human creatures, but all the creatures on the planet — including, presumably, all those lowly crawling things. Moreover, as the flood waters recede, God concludes a covenant, not only with us, but with the whole of creation. The biblical teaching seems to be that the harmony of the spiritual and the physical is what God savors and intends.

The scriptural understanding of the right relationship between the two elements of the person is nowhere better expressed than in St. Mark's laconic account of the temptation of Jesus in the desert. In Mark's telling, we find none of the dramatic details that characterize Matthew's and Luke's narratives. Instead, we have only these sober lines: "He was in the wilderness forty days, tempted by Satan; and he was with the wild beasts and the angels waited on him." This picture of Jesus, surrounded by the animals and ministered to by the angels, is a sort of sacred icon of the right relationship between spirit and matter. It is as though Jesus — in opposition to Satan — brings together, in his person, the warring elements of soul and body, angel and animal. The new Adam, he unites what sin had divided; the new creation, he integrates the cosmic order that sin had disrupted. We shouldn't commune with the angels alone (in the Platonic mode) or with the animals alone (in the hedonist mode); and we certainly shouldn't oscillate back and forth between the two. Rather, we should abide with both, keeping the physical and the spiritual in a mutually correcting harmony. Then we live out our deepest metaphysical identity; then we become the creatures God intended us to be: embodied spirits and spiritual bodies.

Part Four

Holy Men and Women

THE TAX COLLECTOR'S
CONVERSION
Matthew 9:9–13

U NDOUBTEDLY THE MOST FAMOUS STORY of conversion in the New Testament is the account of Saul's
encounter with Christ on the road to Damascus. But
were I venturing a guess as to the second most prominent conversion narrative, I would suggest the story of
the call of Matthew the tax collector. It commences at
chapter 9, verse 9 of the Gospel penned by the convert
himself. I wish to get at this story by looking at it through
a lens provided by a sixteenth-century artist.

Near the Piazza Navona in Rome, there stands the
splendid church of San Luigi dei Francesi, and on the
wall of a dark corner chapel of that edifice there hangs
an unforgettable canvas by the late Renaissance painter
Caravaggio. Caravaggio's Matthew sits at his tax collector's table wearing all of the finery of a sixteenth-century
Italian dandy: silk stockings, jaunty hat, sword at his

side, a feathered cap on his head. (If the artist were alive today, he would most likely depict Matthew wearing an Armani suit, a Rolex watch on his wrist, and Gucci leather shoes on his feet.) Matthew is surrounded by a whole coterie of others who, like him, seem caught up in the superficialities of the high life, and the board at which they sit is piled high with the money that Matthew had extorted from his neighbors and fellow citizens.

Across from the tax collector stands the mysterious figure of Jesus wrapped in shadow. He stretches out his hand and indicates Matthew, who points a finger at his own chest and gazes incredulously at Jesus, as if to say, "You're calling me?" The hand of Caravaggio's Christ might have a familiar aspect, for it is copied from the hand of God the Father in Michelangelo's depiction of the creation of Adam on the Sistine Chapel ceiling. Caravaggio is brilliantly suggesting, not only the divinity of Jesus, but also the quality of conversion as a kind of new creation. Just as the world comes into being through a sheer act of grace, so newness of spiritual life flows, not from the worthiness of the one who receives it, but from the pure generosity of the one who gives it. And as Paul put it in his first letter to Timothy, God wants all people to be saved, even those who, like Matthew, find themselves deeply rooted in a lifestyle inimical to the divine will. If the spiritual life is construed as a game of meriting and deserving, achieving and rewarding, it becomes dysfunctional. It must be thought of as, first and last, a grace joyfully received.

Now what, for us, is that creative and beckoning hand of Jesus? What does it look like? It might be that nagging sense of dissatisfaction, even when we are surrounded with all of the things we thought would make us happy. It might be the voice of a child saying, as a steeple looms into view through the car window, "Why don't we go to church?" It might be that strange and delicious tug we feel in the presence of holy things or holy people. It might be that line from the Scripture that, in an instant, rearranges the furniture of our minds. It might be a weeping willow tree so beautiful that it makes *us* weep. It might be the experience of hitting bottom, a humiliation so profound that our illusions of self-reliance permanently vanish. Although Jesus can call us in many ways, there is a privileged medium of this vocation, and Caravaggio subtly indicates it in his composition. Though his hand and face are arrestingly visible, Jesus is, for the most part, obscured by the body of Peter, who lurches in front of him, interposing himself, as it were, between Christ and the viewer. According to the standard iconography, Peter, the rock and the bearer of the keys, is symbolic of the church. Therefore, Caravaggio is suggesting that it is primarily through the church — the liturgy, the Eucharist, the proclamation of the Scriptures, the summons to moral excellence, the lives of the saints — that we experience the call of Jesus to conversion.

To return to the narrative in Matthew's Gospel, Jesus tells the tax collector, "Follow me." The call of Jesus addresses the mind, to be sure, but it is meant to move through the mind into the body, and through the body into the whole of one's life, into the most practical moves and decisions. "Follow me" has the sense of "apprentice to me" or "walk as I walk; think as I think; choose as I choose; see as I see." Discipleship entails an entire reworking of the self according to the pattern and manner of Jesus. Upon hearing the address of the Lord, Matthew, we are told, "got up and followed him." The Greek word behind "got up" is *anastas,* the same word used to describe the resurrection (*anastasis*) of Jesus from the dead. Following Jesus is indeed a kind of resurrection from the dead, since it involves the transition from a lower form of life to a higher, from a preoccupation with the ephemeral goods of the world to an immersion in the affairs of God. Those who have undergone a profound conversion tend to speak of their former life as a kind of illusion, something not entirely real. Thus Paul can say, "It is no longer I who live, but Christ who lives in me"; Thomas Merton can speak of the "false self" that has given way to the authentic self. And perhaps most movingly, the father of the prodigal son can say, "This son of mine was lost and has been found; he was dead and has come back to life." So is conversion an *anastasis*, a rising from death.

Then the Gospel tells us what happened after Matthew's conversion. "And as he sat at dinner in the house, many tax collectors and sinners came and were sitting with him and his disciples." The first thing that Jesus does, once he calls the sinner to conversion, is invite him to a party! At the very heart of the spiritual life is the conviction that God stands in need of nothing. As I said above, our existence adds nothing to the perfection of God; rather, our existence, in its totality, is a free gift. Therefore, our moral excellence adds nothing to God, and our moral depravity takes nothing from God. What follows from this metaphysical insight is the saving knowledge that God is incapable of playing games of calculation with us. It is not as though we have to "make up for" years of misbehavior in order to be pleasing to God. It is not the case that we have to mollify the hurt feelings of a long-suffering God before he will draw us into his life. The Creator of the universe, the uncaused cause of all of finitude, is always ready to celebrate with us, because he is neither compromised by our sin nor enhanced by our virtue. He *is* nothing but love, right through, and therefore the party is permanently on. All we have to do is respond to the invitation. What sense, then, do we make of all of the scriptural texts having to do with divine anger? As I suggested earlier, those biblical metaphors should be interpreted as expressions of God's passion to set things right. Following Thomas Aquinas, we might say that God is not so much angry for his own sake, but rather for ours. It just annoys him (so to speak) that so many of us are refusing his invitation, constantly extended, to join the fun.

And notice how magnetic the converted Matthew has become! To the party flock all of his fellow tax collectors and other sinners. The call of Jesus has summoned Matthew and through him a whole host of others similarly excluded, by their own self-absorption, from the thrill of the divine life. We can only imagine how rowdy, impolite, and socially questionable this gang of lowlifes is. But there they are, gathered, because of Matthew, around the shepherd of Israel. Whenever I read the account of Matthew's conversion, I'm reminded of the story of Charles Colson, the Watergate conspirator turned Christian evangelist. When he was working for Richard Nixon, Colson said that he would gladly have walked over his grandmother to get the president re-elected. By all accounts, Colson was one of the most ruthless, focused, and morally bankrupt people in the Nixon White House — and that was saying a lot! Then, while he was in prison, Colson experienced, to his in-finite surprise, a radical conversion to Jesus Christ, and for the past thirty-five years, he has been conducting a remarkably successful ministry to prisoners. Christ called this one sinner, and through him, a bevy of others have joined the party.

So it goes in the order of grace.

FALLING IN LOVE
WITH GOD
Luke 1:26–38

THE CHURCH FATHERS saw a vibrant and illuminating connection between Eve, the mother of all the living, and Mary, the mother of God, and it is just this link that the church emphasizes on the feast of the Immaculate Conception, when it juxtaposes the stories of the Fall and the Annunciation. The first reading for that feast is one of the most sacred and important in the tradition, for it narrates the story of what God wants for us and why we find it so hard to acquiesce to the divine desire. Genesis tells us that the Lord created our first parents and placed them in a garden of delights. He then gave them nearly free rein in that paradise. So much attention has been paid over the centuries to the single prohibition that God imposed that we have too easily overlooked the abundantly generous permission: "You may freely eat of every tree of the Garden."

St. Irenaeus expressed the heart of Christian spirituality when he said, *Gloria Dei homo vivens* (the glory of God is a human being fully alive). So many of the gods worshiped by ancient peoples were imagined as rivals to humanity, competitors resentful of our excellence. For instance, in the Greek myth of Prometheus, the god-hero steals precious fire from his fellow gods and spreads it on the earth to the benefit of humankind, but when the gods learn of this theft, they are outraged. They track down Prometheus, tie him to a rock, and send an eagle every day to tear out his liver. In the desperate zero-sum game of human/divine competition, Prometheus had to pay a price for his presumption.

But there is none of this in Christianity. God is not our rival; rather he is the one who rejoices in our being fully alive. God pours out the whole of creation in an effervescent act of generosity, and then, even more surprisingly, he draws his human creatures, through Christ, into the intimacy of friendship with him. We can sense the beginnings of this divine/human friendship in the Genesis account. Adam and Eve at play freely in the field of the Lord represent humanity as God intended: intelligent, creative, engaged, joyfully alive. And in their immersion in all of the delights of Eden we can see the symbolic ground of Catholic humanism, that pleasure that our tradition has taken in philosophy, science, poetry, architecture, and romantic love. There is nothing puritanical in authentic Catholicism, as Hilaire Belloc reminded us in his famous verse:

> Wherever the Catholic sun doth shine,
> There is music and laughter and good red wine.
> At least I have always found it so.
> *Benedicamus Domino.*

But then there is the prohibition: "Of the fruit of the tree in the middle of the Garden you shall not eat lest you die." How do we interpret this command? We certainly know how *not* to read it, because we overhear the interpretation offered by the serpent: "You will not die; God knows that if you eat of this tree, you will be like him, knowing good and evil." What the snake presents is the familiar Promethean reading: God and you are rivals; if you eat of this tree, you will steal something that God is jealously guarding for himself. So says the Father of Lies.

God in fact prohibits the eating of the tree in the middle of the Garden, not because he wants to keep something from his creatures, but because he wants them to fall in love with him. As we have seen, God has nothing against human striving and accomplishing, but God knows that the sweetest experience is had when, at the end of striving, we allow ourselves to be drawn. John Coltrane, the jazz saxophonist, Daniel Barenboim, the

classical pianist, and Eric Clapton, the virtuoso rock gui-
tarist, have all been quoted as saying much the same
thing: my music really comes to life when I stop playing the instrument, and the instrument plays me. When
at the end of his life Thomas Aquinas said that all he
had written seemed as straw compared to what had been
revealed to him, he was not succumbing to despair —
just the contrary. He was surrendering to the ecstasy
beyond what he could possibly attain through his own
efforts. When two people meet and are attracted to
one another, they explore a relationship — analyzing,
conversing, evaluating, sizing one another up. But their
rapport will come to life only when, at the limit of this
process, they *fall* in love with each other, trusting in
a power that transcends whatever they can know and
control on their own.

God wanted our first parents to achieve all they possibly could, but then he wanted them to surrender to
the alluring mystery of the divine life, to fall in love with
him. When they grasped instead, sin entered the world.
And all of the dysfunction of human history — greed,
lust, anger, institutional violence, genocide, meanness of
spirit — has flowed from and been conditioned by that
primordial refusal.

But then, in the fullness of time, in accordance with
God's plan, Mary was conceived without this original sin.

The event of the Immaculate Conception itself is hidden in the privacy of salvation history, but the effect of that event is on display in Luke's account of the Annunciation. The angel announces to the maid of Nazareth that she has been chosen to be the mother of God. In the face of this overwhelming word, Mary is confused: "How is this possible, since I do not know man?" And she cannot begin to imagine the full consequences of accepting this invitation: shame, exile, violent pursuit, the final agony on Calvary. Yet despite her fear and despite the darkness, she says, "I am the maidservant of the Lord; let it be done to me as you say." At the crucial moment, Mary of Nazareth allows herself to fall in love with God, and in that moment of ecstasy the Son of God enters the world for its salvation. The human tragedy began with a grasp; the divine comedy commences with a letting-go. This is why the medieval commentators, with their delicious sense of the co-penetration of all parts of the Bible, observed that the "Ave" of the angel of the Annunciation reverses "Eva," the mother of all the living.

Vatican Council I echoed the great tradition in teaching that God does not need the world, and this is wonderfully good news. For it means that the existence of the universe itself is sheerest grace, the result of God's infinite capacity to fall in love. Salvation, as exemplified in Mary conceived without original sin, is returning the favor.

PETER MAURIN
AND MATTHEW 25
Matthew 25:31–34

W HEN THE RISEN JESUS appeared to Saul on the
road to Damascus, he said, "Saul, Saul, why
are you persecuting me?" Reasonably enough, Saul won-
dered who this mysterious interlocutor might be: "Who
are you, sir?" The answer came: "I am Jesus whom you
are persecuting." Saul of Tarsus had never met Jesus of
Nazareth, but he was actively hunting down those who
claimed Jesus as the Messiah of Israel. This exchange on
the Damascus road, therefore, reveals something peculiar and distinctive about our Catholic ecclesiology. Jesus
so radically identifies with his body the church, with his
people, that an attack on them is tantamount to an attack on him. The same motif is on display in the famous
passage from the twenty-fifth chapter of Matthew's Gospel, wherein Jesus anticipates the terrible day when he
will appear as judge of all the nations, separating the

sheep from the goats. He tells the righteous that they had cared for him in his hour of need, giving him food when he was hungry and drink when he was thirsty. Puzzled, they ask, "When, Lord, did we do all these things for you?" And he answers, "Amen I say to you, whatever you did for one of the least brothers of mine, you did for me." The King *is* the least of his people; and therefore kindness to them is kindness to him.

Peter Maurin was a Christian who felt the truth of this ecclesiology in his bones. He was born in May of 1877 in the south of France, one of twenty-three children. In his early years, he was educated by the Christian Brothers and became, through them, deeply inspired by the example of St. Francis of Assisi. In 1909, soon after the French government became officially hostile to the church, he sailed for North America and settled eventually in Canada. For about twenty years, he lived a sort of radical Franciscan life, performing manual labor during the day, sleeping by night in any bed he could find, and dining in skid-row beaneries. He made a little extra money in those days, offering courses in the French language, but whatever surplus funds he garnered he immediately gave away to those less fortunate than he. Maurin was, from his youth, deeply interested in the life of the mind, and during these vagabond years, he was struggling to develop a coherent Catholic social philosophy — a theory of economics and politics thoroughly informed by Christian doctrine. The principal problem with modern society, he thought, was that the social life had become all but divorced from the moral imperatives of the Gospel. For most Christians, religion was a private matter, having no discernable effect on the way the political and social order was conducted. But the result of this privatization was that society had effectively lost its transcendent purpose. Economic life had come to be organized around the drive for productivity and the quest for profits, rather than around the spiritual cultivation of the person. That Maurin's concern perhaps strikes us as peculiar is a testament to how thoroughly modern we have become, for in the classical Christian tradition, the form of politics is indeed morality. According to Thomas Aquinas (to cite just one Christian authority among many), the purpose of social life is to foster the common good and to make each participant in civil society a better person, which is to say, more completely ordered to God. This is the social philosophy that Peter Maurin had absorbed from his reading and that he was trying to revive for his own time.

He saw that at the root of Catholic social teaching was the passage from Matthew 25 we considered above. The radical identification of Christ with his suffering body, with the poor and forgotten and destitute, was "dynamite," power, for it implied that the worship of Jesus must lead to societal transformation. The trouble is, Maurin said, that "the church has taken its own dynamite, placed it in hermetically sealed containers, and sat on the lids." Once Matthew 25 was taken seriously, no Christian could, with moral consistency, come to prayer on Sunday and remain indifferent to the social structures that permitted millions to live in poverty and subhuman conditions. Maurin's program amounted to what he called "a personalist revolution," a changing of the structures of society from within through the gradual conversion of individual Christians to the vision of Matthew 25. The believer in Jesus, he stated, should simply begin living now according to a new set of values: "The future will be different only if we make the present different." He wanted to change modern America from being "a society of go-getters to a society of go-givers." And how should one go about making this change? By following, Maurin taught, the practical precepts of the church, which flow directly from Matthew 25 — namely, the corporal and spiritual works of mercy: feed the hungry, give drink to the thirsty, clothe the naked, visit the imprisoned, shelter the homeless, bury the dead, counsel the doubtful, instruct the ignorant, pray for the living and the dead. When these are practiced, one's concern for "peace and justice" is no longer an abstraction or a vague inclination. When the Christian makes these central to her spiritual life, she "blows up some of the dynamite of the church."

In 1932, just as the Great Depression was getting under way, Peter Maurin found himself in New York City. There he met a young woman, a spiritual seeker and social activist who had just converted to Catholicism. Her name was Dorothy Day. Dorothy was struggling to find a way to bring her passion for social justice together with her passion for the life of prayer, and a mutual friend had suggested that she and Maurin meet. She said later that, at their first encounter, Peter talked nonstop for seven hours! Despite his loquaciousness, she was entranced by the vagabond philosopher, the radical Catholic who quite clearly embodied what he preached. Peter told her that she must found a newspaper that would present Catholic social teaching and open a house of hospitality where the works of mercy could be concretely practiced and where Peter could engage in "clarification of thought."

And this is precisely what she did. Together Day and Maurin founded the Catholic Worker movement, at the heart of which lay a newspaper and houses of hospitality.

Read Dorothy Day's wonderful autobiographical reflections to get a feel for the early days of the movement, when the staffing of breadlines, the making of gallons of bean soup, frequent retreats and benedictions, Peter's all-night philosophy sessions, and the comings and goings of sometimes saintly and sometimes dangerous homeless people all came together in a more or less grace-filled melange.

Soon after the founding of the movement, Peter began to accept speaking invitations and traveled around the country, spreading the Gospel of the Catholic Worker. Stories abound about his hobo ways during these lecture trips. On one occasion, a formal greeting committee had gathered at a railway station where Maurin was expected to arrive. His train came and went, and there was no sign of their celebrated speaker. Looking rather desperately around the platform, they caught sight of a homeless man sleeping on a bench and using a newspaper as a crude blanket. They woke him, hoping that he might have seen their lost lecturer. It was Peter. He had arrived on an earlier train and had simply made himself at home. By the end of his lecturing career, he had become so absent-minded and so oblivious to practicalities that Dorothy arranged to pin a small sign to his suit, reading, "I am Peter Maurin, founder of the Catholic Worker Movement."

Though Christians of good will can work out the details in different ways, no Christian, it seems to me, can overlook what Peter Maurin so clearly saw: that we simply cannot love Christ without concretely loving those most in need. Though there are relatively conservative and relatively progressive ways to blow things up, no Christian can fail to acknowledge the political and economic dynamite implied in the twenty-fifth chapter of Matthew's Gospel. Maurin taught that we take nothing here below with us when we die. We leave behind our wealth, our earthly power, our social status, our degrees, and our titles. But, in his own words, "What we give to the poor for Christ's sake is what we carry with us when we die."

TU ES PETRUS

Matthew 16:13–19

I N THE SIXTEENTH CHAPTER of Matthew's Gospel, we hear that Jesus, having come into the district of Caesarea Philippi, asked his disciples a peculiar question: "Who do people say that the Son of Man is?" We could easily imagine the Buddha asking his followers, "What do people think about my teaching?" Or Muhammad wondering, "What do the crowds make of the revelation that was given to me?" Or Confucius inquiring whether the leaders of his society found his ethical system compelling. But it would be counterintuitive to imagine any of them asking, "Who do people say that I *am?*"

No self-respecting Buddhist today thinks that the ontology of the Buddha is a matter of great importance, and no honest contemporary Muslim spends even a moment investigating the metaphysical make-up of Muhammad. And yet Jesus does not ask what the people think of his doctrine or his words or his behavior. He asks what they think about his *person*. And this distinctive question has been stubbornly posed and answered up and down the Christian centuries to this day. During the first several centuries of the church's life, fierce intellectual battles were fought over how to understand Jesus' being and essence, and every time we recite the Nicene Creed at liturgy today, we rehearse the classic resolution of this debate: he is "God from God, light from light, true God from true God, begotten not made, one in being with the Father." Knowing who Jesus *is* matters desperately for Christians.

As this section of Matthew's sixteenth chapter unfolds, we hear a range of answers to Jesus' surprising question. The disciples report, first, what the average person is saying, what the common consensus is: "Some say John the Baptist, others Elijah, still others Jeremiah or one of the prophets." We can only imagine the electric effect that Jesus the charismatic healer and compelling preacher was having on the people of his time and place. There must have been a buzz around him similar to that surrounding celebrities and pop stars today. Excited assessments and comparisons must have been circulating in the crowds that followed him, and this is what we hear in the disciples' report. What is worth noting is that all of it is *wrong*. Were we to ask "the people" today, through public opinion surveys, who Jesus is, we should expect a similar range of views — prophet, teacher, guru, madman, religious founder. And these, too, would be inadequate. Though this cuts painfully against our democratic instincts, the correct knowledge concerning the identity of Jesus does not come from the people; it does not emerge gradually and through consensus from below. It does not flow, in the manner of political truth, from the sifting and weighing of varying perspectives. To be sure, in regard to practical, prudential judgments, this democratic consensus-building model might be applicable in the church, but with regard to the determination of the central matter, it must cede place to something else.

So Jesus, having surveyed the general attitude, turns his attention to his inner circle: "But who do you say that I am?" We should expect a better answer from this narrower constituency, these intimate friends who were chosen by Jesus: the ones who had watched him at close quarters over the course of many months; who had, we presume, listened attentively to his preaching; who had seen the mighty works he had done. Surely they will give a more adequate response. But the college of disciples doesn't speak. Are they intimidated by the question? Are they ashamed of their ignorance? It is not clear. What is evident is that they aren't any more reliable than the people. It is said often enough that the church is not a democracy (which is essentially true), but it's not frequently remarked that neither is the church an aristocracy. Classical philosophers such as Plato, Aristotle, Pythagoras, and Cicero were not great advocates of what we'd call representative democracy; rather, they called for rule by the best and brightest, the sophisticated elite. Much of Plato's *Republic*, for instance, is devoted to an account of how the aristocratic class ought to be educated in order to prepare them for their careers as philosopher-kings. It might seem that, even though their flaws are on rather full display in the Gospels, the twelve apostles would qualify as a Christian version of such an aristocracy, a college of the best-informed and most fully initiated. But they don't have the answer.

Finally Simon Peter speaks: "You are the Christ, the Son of the living God." Peter confesses that Jesus is the *Meschiach,* the anointed one, the long-awaited Davidic savior, the person to whom the whole of the Hebrew Scriptures pointed. But his confession is even more startling, for he affirms that Jesus is not simply a human hero, or a religious teacher of surpassing wisdom, nor even the greatest man who ever lived. He claims that Jesus is somehow else, qualitatively different from anyone who came before or who would come after; he is the Son of the living God. This is the mystical insight that stands at the heart of Christianity. To hold this Petrine faith is to be a Christian; to deny it is to be not a Christian.

After Peter's confession, we hear Jesus speak: "Blessed are you, Simon son of Jonah. For flesh and blood has not revealed this to you, but my heavenly Father." The implication here is that Simon's insight did not come from his own intelligent speculation, nor from consultation with his apostolic colleagues, nor from the consensus of the people. It did not come, in a word, from flesh and blood, but rather from above, through grace, from God. And this is why Simon needs a new name: "And I say to you that you are Peter and upon this rock I will build my church." Jesus would have called him *Kepha* in Aramaic, which is rendered in Greek as *Petros* and hence "Peter" in English. The nickname means, essentially, "rocky," and the recognition of the charismatic nature of Rocky's confession has been a defining mark of the Catholic Church ever since that day at Caesarea Philippi.

After the election of Benedict XVI as pope in April of 2005, the cardinals who had chosen him gathered on the loggia overlooking St. Peter's Square. The news cameras caught the remarkably pensive look on the face of Cardinal Francis George of Chicago, and many reporters asked him, upon his return, what he had been musing about that evening. Cardinal George said that, as he looked out over the city of Rome, he caught sight of the Circus Maximus, where Roman emperors had once watched Christian martyrs going to their death. And he was thinking, "Where is Nero's successor? Or Trajan's or Marcus Aurelius's? And finally, who cares?" The cardinal went on: "But if you want to see Peter's successor, he is right over there, smiling and waving to the crowds. I was thinking," he said, "about the enduring quality of the church built on Peter's faith."

He is right, of course. Nations, cultures, and institutions have come and gone, but the church remains; the Roman civilization has disappeared; the Byzantine empire has drifted away; Charlemagne's kingdom broke apart long ago; Napoleon's government, the Russia of the Tsars, Stalin's Communist state, Hitler's thousand-year Reich — they've all passed into history. But the church, founded on Peter's confession, is still, strangely, here. Of course, we shouldn't be too surprised, for we have the guarantee of Jesus himself: "The gates of the netherworld shall not prevail against it."

After his confession, Peter receives not only a new name, but also a gift: "I will give you the keys of the kingdom of heaven." G. K. Chesterton commented that a key is both oddly shaped and hard, precisely because it is designed reliably to open, over a long period of time, a very definitely shaped lock. Peter's mystical intuition regarding the identity of Jesus has developed over the centuries into a densely elaborated theology and creedal

151

system, filled with complexities, puzzling twists, and unexpected emphases. This is because, like a key, it is meant to correspond to a subtly configured lock, the one fitted into the door to the kingdom of heaven. And this system, however complexly articulated, remains hard, firm, reliable — for what good is that key if it loses its shape?

The church rests, thank God, not on the shifting sands of popular opinion, nor on the learned speculation of an intellectual elite, but rather on Rocky and his successors down through the ages, who know who Jesus is and who hold stubbornly on to those keys.

Part Five

Liturgy and Prayer

THE MYSTERY OF THE MASS
John 6:1–15

THE SIXTH CHAPTER of John's Gospel is a master-piece within the masterpiece. The entire Gospel of John is of great literary sophistication and is rich in mystical associations, but the sixth chapter is especially dense, evocative, and symbolically charged. One of the distinctive features of the fourth Gospel is that, unlike the Synoptic Gospels, it does not include an "institution narrative," an account of the words that Jesus spoke over the bread and wine at the Last Supper. But this does not mean that the Eucharist is absent in John. In fact, some scholars suggest that the entire Gospel is suffused with the Eucharist — that in a sense, the whole text is an indirect commentary on Jesus' body and blood. Though that might be a bit of an exaggeration, there is no question that John's sixth chapter constitutes a sustained and intense meditation on the meaning of the Eucharist. And this is why, every third summer, the church's lectionary invites us to read this section of the fourth Gospel with particular care and attention.

At the center of chapter 6 is the magnificent bread-of-life discourse that Jesus proclaims at the synagogue of Capharnaum, but the chapter opens with an account of the multiplication of the loaves and fishes. John's presentation of this miracle is an implicit theology of the Mass, for the liturgy is the context in which the Eucharist is most appropriately situated. Mind you, by the time that John's Gospel was composed (toward the end of the first century), the eucharistic liturgy was already well established within the primitive Christian communities. Here we find one of its earliest and finest theological elaborations.

We hear first that Jesus went up a mountain and sat down there with his disciples. Throughout the Bible, mountains function as symbols of the encounter between God and humanity. They are the places where humans go up and God, as it were, comes down to meet them. Thus, Mt. Ararat is the spot where Noah's ark comes to rest and where one of the first sacrifices in salvation history occurs; Mt. Sinai, wreathed in smoke, is where the law is given; Mt. Tabor provides the setting for the Transfiguration of the Lord, a kind of window into the transcendent dimension; and Mt. Calvary is the place where the ultimate reconciliation between the holy God and sinful humanity is effected. So the Mass is a mountaintop experience, a privileged encounter. Notwithstanding a great deal of inadequate postconciliar catechesis, the liturgy is not simply a celebration of the worshiping community; nor is it, primarily, the gathering of a club of richly diverse people. It is, first and foremost, a communion with the living God, a participation, even now, in the life of heaven.

We might rather easily overlook the detail of Jesus sitting down, but it is significant. In the ancient world, sitting was the posture of the teacher. Our expression "sitting at the feet of a master" calls to mind the attitude of students who would arrange themselves on the ground, looking up to the seated teacher. Therefore, when Jesus is described as sitting in the company of his disciples (learners), we are, as it were, in the ancient classroom or the place of instruction. Much the same thing is signaled, incidentally, in the fifth chapter of Matthew when we read that Jesus went up another mountain and sat down to deliver his definitive teaching, the Sermon on the Mount. In the symbolic context of our Johannine scene, it signifies the liturgy of the word, the first part of the Mass in which the Sacred Scriptures are read. The Vatican II documents clearly indicate that when the Bible is proclaimed at the liturgy, it is Christ himself who is teaching through the words and gestures of the readers. During this portion of the liturgy, we are all learners, disciples at the feet of the master teacher. In the Emmaus story, from the twenty-fourth chapter of Luke's Gospel, we find a very similar symbolic association: as they walk together, the risen Jesus explains the Scriptures to his dejected disciples, and their hearts are enlivened.

Next, St. John tells us that "the Jewish feast of Passover was near." None of the details of time or number should be overlooked in this subtle Gospel. On John's telling, the death of Jesus took place on the day before Passover, at the time when the lambs were being slaughtered in preparation for the great feast. This juxtaposition is meant to indicate that Jesus himself is the Lamb of God, whose sacrifice would inaugurate the passover from sin to eternal life. Placing this scene from chapter 6 on the eve of Passover, therefore, effects a connection between the Eucharist and the dying of the Lord. What happens in the second major section of the Mass is a re-presentation of the sacrifice of Calvary, a sacramental realization of the self-offering of the Lamb of God. Thus, this reminder of the timing of the event signals the transition from the liturgy of the word to the liturgy of the Eucharist, from the instruction to the sacrifice.

Seeing the vast crowd before him, Jesus asks his disciple Philip, "Where can we buy enough food for them to eat?" It is a biblical commonplace that God, who needs nothing in order to achieve his will, nevertheless delights in inviting human cooperation in his endeavors. Andrew comments, "There is a boy here who has five barley loaves and two fish." These simple elements stand for what human beings can bring in order to realize the purposes of God, and thus they are evocative of the humble gifts that are presented at the offertory of the Mass: bread, wine, and water. None of this, of course, can even begin to satisfy the hunger that gnaws at the depth of our souls, but Christ wants it and uses it.

Then we hear that "Jesus took the loaves and gave thanks." At the Mass, the priest operates and speaks, not in his own name, but rather *in persona Christi,* in the very person of Jesus. The first words that he utters in Jesus' name over the gifts are an expression of thanksgiving: "Blessed are you, Lord God of all creation, for through your goodness we have these gifts to offer." Then, in the great eucharistic (thanksgiving) prayer, he pronounces the Last Supper words of Jesus over the bread and wine: "This is my body; this is the cup of my blood." In so doing, he elevates and transforms those simple substances into the body and blood of Jesus, into the divine life that is alone capable of satisfying the hungry heart. In the same way, Christ can elevate and expand whatever contribution of mind, passion, and will that we offer to him.

The Johannine story anticipates and echoes this move when it tells of the multiplication of the meager gifts for the feeding of the crowd: "They had as much as they wanted." From beginning to end of the Bible, in narratives, poems, doctrines, and psalms, we hear the lesson that nothing in the creaturely realm — food, sex, power, esteem, pleasure — can finally satisfy the longing for the infinite that is an essential feature of the human spirit. Only in God are our souls at rest. The sated five thousand, those who have "had their fill," are therefore symbolic of the participants in the Mass who have received the body and blood of the Lord. We speak of the obligation of attending the liturgy and of the mortal sin involved in consciously missing it. We should think of this not so much legalistically as organically. One is obliged to attend the Mass in the same way that one is obliged to eat and drink: as the essential condition of life. Why must we participate in the liturgy? Because that is where the lifeblood of God is on offer.

There is one more symbolic connection we should make. John tells us that, at the conclusion of the meal, they gathered the fragments that were left over and "they filled twelve wicker baskets." How redolent this is of the liturgy, at the end of which the faithful gather up and preserve the elements that remain. Once again, we should not overlook the importance of numbers. The twelve baskets call to mind the twelve tribes of Israel, the holy people that Jesus was sent to gather. The eucharistic assembly has an eschatological overtone — it is meant to evoke the fulfillment of all things at the end of time. At the Mass, we are communing, not only with those who are physically proximate to us, but also, in Christ, with the angels, the saints, and all of the saved.

On the holy mountain, Jesus teaches, receives humble gifts, and uses them to feed the crowds. This is the Mass, in your parish on a Tuesday morning and in heaven before the throne of God.

THE RULES OF PRAYER
Mark 11:20–25

HOW SHOULD WE PRAY? What makes prayer ef-
ficacious? Why does it seem that some prayers
are answered and others are not? How does prayer
"work"? These are questions that come, not simply from
theoreticians of religion, but from religious people, ordinary believers. Studies indicate that we are a nation
of pray-ers, yet we struggle rather mightily with the
mechanics, meaning, and practicalities of prayer. The
Bible, of course, witnesses constantly to the centrality of prayer. What binds together figures as diverse as
Noah, Moses, Jacob, Abraham, Jeremiah, Daniel, King
Hezekiah, Queen Esther, Peter, and Paul is that they all
pray — and not provisionally, occasionally, or perfuncto-
rily, but consistently and as an expression of their deepest
selves. And, of course, Jesus prays and famously teaches
his disciples to pray.

162

Taking a cue from the contemporary spiritual writer Anthony de Mello, I would like to share four "rules" of prayer. These are not the elements of an airtight formula ("follow these and your prayer will be answered"), but rather powerful and consistent indications regarding the practice of prayer, coming from the biblical texts and refined by the great tradition.

Rule one: you must pray with faith. Have you noticed how, time and again, Jesus says to people before he works a miracle, "Do you believe that I can do this?" Matthew tells us that, on one occasion, Jesus was unable to perform many healings in a given place because he met with so little faith among the people there. And Luke reports this word of the Lord: "I tell you this, if only you had faith and have no doubts, you need only say to the mountain, 'Be lifted from your place and hurled into the sea,' and what you say will be done." After Bartimaeus receives his sight, Jesus says to him, "Go, your faith has saved you." There are many Christians today, working in the healing ministries, who seem able, through the simplicity and integrity of their trust, to produce miraculous effects after the manner of Jesus himself. How can we explain this correlation between faith and the answering of prayer? Again, we should never think of this in an automatic way, since we are always dealing with the freedom and sovereignty of God. Nevertheless, we might suggest the following connection. God's grace and loving-kindness are neither manipulative nor domineering; instead, they require, by God's design, the conduit of a receptive freedom in order to be realized into our lives. It is a commonplace of Catholic theology that God is always pleased to work in cooperation with our powers of will and mind. Faith, therefore, is this conduit, this open door; it is a signal, coming from the depths of our existence, that we want to cooperate with grace. We might, therefore, follow the extraordinary advice that Jesus offers in the eleventh chapter of Mark's Gospel: "So I tell you, whatever you ask for in prayer, believe that you have received it, and it will be yours." In other words, let your faith be so pure and strong that you easily believe that you already have what you have asked God to give you — and you may find that you do indeed receive it.

A second rule of prayer is this: if you want your prayer answered, forgive. There is an exhortation of the Lord, found in the Gospel of Matthew, that, over the centuries, has conditioned the liturgical practice of the church: "If when you are bringing your gift to the altar, you suddenly remember that your brother has a grievance against you, leave your gift before the altar. First go and make peace with your brother." And in that same eleventh chapter of Mark that we considered above, there is this piece of blunt advice: "And when you stand praying, if you have a grievance against anyone, forgive him, so that your Father in heaven may forgive you." In both cases, Jesus seems to imply, if not a strict causal connection, at least a correspondence between answered prayer and the reconciliation of differences. It appears as though effective prayer is simply incompatible with the nursing of grudges and the bearing of resentments.

Why should this be the case? Again, it is impossible to respond with anything like demonstrable certitude, but we might suggest that it has something to do with the nature of God. When one prays, one is asking, essentially, for some participation in the life of God. But God *is* love. Therefore, to remain in an act or attitude that contradicts love would, it seems, place an obstacle in the way of grace. If some decent request of yours is being stubbornly refused, look at the quality of your relationships and see if there is not something there that is repugnant to the nature of the God you are petitioning.

A third rule of prayer, on display throughout the biblical witness, is to pray with perseverance. We see this in that wonderful Genesis account of Abraham dickering with God over the destruction of Sodom: "Suppose there are fifty righteous within the city. . . . Suppose forty are found there. . . . Suppose ten are found there." With a sort of sacred chutzpah, Abraham stands in the presence of God and stubbornly, persistently asks for what he wants. And in one of Jesus' parables, we hear of a man who knocks at his neighbor's door only to be told that the neighbor and his wife are in bed and cannot be bothered. He knocks again and again, until finally, in exasperation, the neighbor relents and gives the petitioner what he seeks. This story is, of course, followed by Jesus' unambiguous teaching: "Knock and it shall be opened to you; seek and you will find; ask and it will be given to you." It appears as though one reason we don't receive what we want through prayer is that we give up far too easily. St. Augustine said that God sometimes delays in giving us what we desire because he wants our hearts to expand through anticipation. Precisely when we are refused, our ardor grows and our desire increases so as to receive the fullness of what God desires for us. This process is short-circuited when, in our frustration at not being answered promptly, we cease to ask.

A fourth and final rule of prayer, embodied, like rule two, in the liturgical tradition of the Christian churches, is this: pray in Jesus' name. The ground for this rule is in the explicit statement of Christ: "Anything you ask in my name I will do, so that the Father may be glorified in the Son. If you ask anything in my name, I will do it." When we pray in the name of Jesus, we are relying on his intimacy with the Father, trusting that the Father will listen to his Son who pleads on our behalf. In the letter to the

Hebrews, we hear that Jesus, like us in all things but sin, a fellow sufferer with us, has entered as our advocate into the heavenly court. Risking a crude comparison, it is as though Jesus is our man in city hall, a representative for us in the place of ultimate power. Just as a lowly petitioner in Washington might get his senator's attention by dropping the name of an influential acquaintance, so we Christians confidently mention the name of Jesus while petitioning at the throne of the Father. Mind you, this analogy is limited: the Father must not be construed as a reluctant and distracted executive, annoyed by the petty appeals of his constituents, mediated by a persistent lobbyist. For the author of the letter to the Hebrews, Jesus has become our advocate, precisely because the Father wanted him to assume this role for us; and therefore, presumably, the Father delights in hearing us call upon him through his Son.

There is another dimension to this rule. Invoking the name of Jesus is an effective way to monitor the quality and to shape the content of our prayer. When we pray "through Christ our Lord," we are assuming the stance and attitude of Jesus, aligning ourselves to him, compelling ourselves to desire what he desires. Accordingly, it is altogether consistent to pray in the name of Jesus for peace, for justice, for the forgiveness of our enemies, for greater faith, or for the health of those we love. Those are all goods that Jesus would want. But how anomalous it would be to pray for vengeance against our enemies in Jesus' name, or for a Maserati through Christ our Lord!

Therefore, follow the rules of prayer: pray with faith; pray in conjunction with acts of forgiveness; pray with persistence; and pray in the name of Jesus.

REAL PRESENCE
John 6:48–66

T HE MOST CHALLENGING SERMON that Jesus ever preached was not the Sermon on the Mount; it was the discourse he gave in the Capharnaum synagogue after the miracle of multiplying the loaves and fishes. The Sermon on the Mount — with its calls for love of one's enemy, the cleansing of the interior self, and nonresistance to evil — was certainly intellectually confounding. But the talk that Jesus gave at Capharnaum concerning the sacrament of his body and blood was not only philosophically problematic; it was, quite literally, revolting. Even at a distance of two thousand years and after volumes of theological reflection, readers today can still find his words awfully hard to accept. We can tolerate easily enough the claim that Jesus is a spiritual teacher of great importance; we might even accept that his person is central in regard to our relation to God. But that his flesh is real food and his blood real drink? That the ingesting of

169

these elements is essential to gaining eternal life? Even the most sympathetic of contemporary listeners is likely to react the same way many in Jesus' original audience reacted: with a shake of the head and perhaps even a shudder of disgust.

To understand why Jesus' own hearers would have responded in a particularly negative way to these words, we must remember the clear and repeated prohibitions in the Hebrew Scriptures against the consuming of flesh and blood. In Genesis 9:4, we find this: "Every moving thing that lives shall be food for you...but you shall not eat flesh with its life, that is, its blood." In Leviticus 3:17, we read, "It shall be a perpetual statute throughout your generations: you must not eat any fat or any blood." And in Deuteronomy 12:23, we discover, "The clean and the unclean alike you may eat; only be sure you do not eat the blood." Finally, the expression "to eat someone's flesh" was commonly used in Jesus' time to designate the most vicious and unwarranted kind of attack. Therefore, when Jesus says, "I am the living bread that came down from heaven;...the bread that I will give for the life of the world is my flesh," he is implying something about as nauseating and religiously objectionable as possible. It is, accordingly, a rather remarkable understatement when John writes, "The Jews then disputed among themselves saying, 'How can this man give us his flesh to eat?'"

So what does Jesus do when confronted with this objection? One would think that, in order to mollify his opponents, he would take the opportunity to soften his rhetoric, to offer a metaphorical or symbolic interpretation of his words, so as at least to answer the most obvious difficulties. Instead, he intensifies what he had said: "Amen, amen I say to you, unless you eat the flesh of the Son of Man and drink his blood, you do not have life within you." The Greek term translated here by "eat" is not the usual *phagein* but rather *trogein*, a word customarily used to describe the way animals devour their food. We might render it "gnaw" or "chomp." Therefore, to those who are revolted by the realism of his language, Jesus says, essentially, "Unless you gnaw on my flesh...you have no life in you."

How do we appropriate this shocking talk? If we stand in the great Catholic tradition, we honor these unnerving words of Jesus, resisting all attempts to soften them or explain them away. We affirm what the church has come to call the doctrine of the "real presence." Vatican II reexpressed the traditional Catholic belief when it taught that, though Jesus is present to us in any number of ways — in the proclamation of the Gospel, in the gathering of two or three in his name, in the person of the priest at the liturgy, in the poor and suffering — he is nevertheless present in a qualitatively different way in the Eucharist. In the consecrated elements, he is "really, truly, and substantially" present to us; that is to say, his very self — body and blood, humanity and divinity — is offered to us under the form of bread and wine. Thomas Aquinas expressed this difference as follows: though in all of the other sacraments the power of Christ is present, in the Eucharist *ipse Christus*, Christ himself is present. And this is why, for Catholics, the Eucharist is not one sign among many, one inspiring symbol among others. It is the very soul and life of the church, the hinge upon which the life of the church turns. The centrality of the Eucharist to the life of the community was pithily summed up in the title of John Paul II's last encyclical, *Ecclesia de Eucharistia* (the church comes from the Eucharist).

But still, what prevents us from walking away from this teaching? How can our reaction to this doctrine — however ecclesially important it may be — be anything but that of the first people who heard it? Let me open up one avenue of explanation. Depending upon the circumstances and the authority of the speaker, human words can change reality. If I were to walk up to you at a party and say, "You're under arrest," you would ignore me or perhaps assume I was starting a joke. But if a uniformed and properly deputed police officer came to your door and said those same words, you would, in fact, be under arrest. Or if I, from the vantage point of my box seat, were to shout out "safe" as Derek Jeter slid into third base, my exclamation would have no objective effect; but if the properly designated American League umpire, stationed just outside of the third-base foul line, shouted, "You're out" as Jeter slid in, the unfortunate Yankee would be, in point of fact, out. Further, a word of praise uttered by a beloved professor can start a student on the career path that will determine his life; and a word of criticism from a parent can wound so deeply that a child never recovers emotionally. The point is this: even our puny words can, to a greater or lesser degree, change reality.

Now consider the divine word. According to the author of Genesis, God spoke and things came into being. "Let there be light, and there was light; let the earth bring forth living creatures of every kind ... and it was so; let us make humankind in our image, according to our likeness ... so God created humankind in his image." And in the fifty-fifth chapter of the book of the prophet Isaiah, we find this extraordinary divine assertion: "As the rain and the snow come down from heaven and do not return there until they have watered the earth ... so shall my word be that goes out from my mouth; it shall not return to me empty, but it shall accomplish that which I purpose." God's word, on the biblical telling, is not so much descriptive as creative. It does not express a state of affairs that already exists; it makes a state of affairs to be. God's word speaks things into existence, determining them at the deepest roots of their being. And doesn't St. John express this idea in the prologue to his Gospel? "In the beginning was the Word, and the Word was with God and the Word was God.... All things came into being through him, and without him nothing came into being."

Who is Jesus but this creative Word of God made flesh? Therefore, what Jesus says, is. If he were merely a powerful preacher or prophet, his words could affect reality only superficially, as we saw in the examples above. But he is more than a prophet, more than a teacher. On the night before he died, Jesus took bread, said the blessing, broke it, and gave it to his disciples, saying, "Take this all of you and eat it, this is my body." In the same way, after the meal, he took the cup filled with wine. Giving thanks, he passed the cup to his friends and said, "Take this all of you and drink from it; this is the cup of my blood." Given who he is, these words bore the creative power of the Logos of God. They effected a change, therefore, not simply at the level of symbolic or metaphorical reconfiguration; instead, they pierced to the very roots of the existence of those elements and changed them into something else, into his body and blood. In his great treatise on the Eucharist, Thomas Aquinas appropriately compares this "substantial" change to the act of creation, since both are based upon the unique power of the divine Word.

This change, this transubstantiation, explains why the church comes from the Eucharist and why eternal life comes from eating the Lord's body and drinking his blood.

PRIEST, PEOPLE, AND RITE
Revelation 4:1–11

S QUINTED AT THEOLOGICALLY, the twentieth century was, in many ways, the century of the liturgy. Some of the greatest figures in preconciliar Catholic thought — Hans Urs von Balthasar, Romano Guardini, Virgil Michel, Henri de Lubac — were preoccupied with the meaning of the Mass; the Vatican II fathers, of course, put liturgy at the very center of their concerns; and Joseph Ratzinger — now Pope Benedict XVI — has written extensively on the subject over the course of five decades. All of this intellectual and spiritual effort has produced, for us, a deepened and clarified vision of the mystery of the liturgy. Let us reflect on the Mass along the lines suggested by Msgr. M. Francis Mannion, a worthy successor to the great figures just mentioned and a bearer of their tradition.

Mannion argues that there are three elements required for authentic liturgy: the priest, the people, and

176

the ritual. The Mass is, at least normatively, a dynamic and interdependent play of these three dimensions. Let us look, first, at the priest. A Catholic Mass requires the presence of a validly ordained minister of the church who has been empowered to interpret the Word of Scripture and to effect the change of bread and wine into the body and blood of Jesus. Without a priest, a service can be rich, powerful, moving, religiously uplifting — but it can't be a eucharistic liturgy. Why is the ordained priest so central? First, he is a link to the bishop, who ordained him and/or assigned him, and through the bishop to the bishop of Rome, who is the visible sign of the unity of the body of Christ around the world.

This is not primarily a juridical claim, but a sacramental and symbolic one. The Mass does indeed take place in a local setting, but its contours and purpose are really universal, for its words and gestures are shared throughout the mystical body of Jesus. The priest is the guarantor of this universality, the sure sign that a particular community has overcome a tendency toward self-preoccupation.

Secondly, the priest is the one who has the unique capacity to operate *in persona Christi,* in the very person of Christ. As such, when he speaks the words of the Lord over the bread and wine — "this is my body; this is the cup of my blood" — they effect what they say, since they are the speech of Christ, the Logos through which all things are created. For the biblical authors, as we saw earlier, God's word is not so much descriptive as productive. It does not simply inform us of a state of affairs; it constitutes a state of affairs. Therefore, the priest, operating as an instrumental cause, makes Christ to be really, truly, and substantially present to his people. Robert Sokolowski has contended that a priest wears vestments at Mass and submits to the discipline of a ritual precisely because he is meant to subordinate his particular personality to Christ. The Eucharistic consecration — during which Christ speaks his own words through the words of the priest — is but the most concentrated expression of this liturgical subordination.

Next, according to Mannion, authentic liturgy requires the people, the congregation. Cardinal John Henry Newman was once asked to comment on the role of the laity in the church, and he responded, "Well, the church would look pretty silly without them!" And so the liturgy — the source and summit of the church's life — would look pretty silly without the people. An oft-stated conviction of the preconciliar liturgical theologians was that the congregation at Mass should never be construed as spectators at a clerical event, as though the liturgy belonged essentially to the priest and only incidentally to them. Rather, they taught, priest and congregation participate together in the liturgy, each in a distinctive manner and each organically ordered to the other. In point of fact, in their words, gestures, posture, prayer, and song, the laity act out their baptismally grounded priestly identity. All of this theologizing came to expression in Vatican II's famous call for the "full, conscious, and active participation" of the congregation in the liturgy.

What if one were to object that since a priest may celebrate an entirely valid Mass privately, the people cannot be an essential element in the liturgical whole? Well, in fact, there is no such thing as a "private" Mass, for every liturgy here below participates dynamically in the heavenly liturgy, the worship that the angels and saints give continually to God. So even when the priest says Mass in the privacy of his chapel, he is intensely involved with an unseen congregation. The community — whether living or dead, whether natural or supernatural — matters.

Third, Mannion maintains, liturgy requires the ritual. The Mass is not a free-floating prayer form by which the gathered community expresses their spiritual feelings; it is, rather, a series of carefully prescribed prayers, movements, gestures, and ritual actions. When the newly ordained Thomas Merton was asked by a non-Catholic friend to explain the meaning of the Mass, Merton said that it was like a ballet, a tightly circumscribed sacred dance. As a ritual, the Mass is something like the text

179

of a Shakespearean play or the score of a Beethoven symphony. Though we allow a director a fair amount of creative range, we would, I imagine, be mightily displeased if he played fast and loose with the text of *King Lear*. So the liturgy, in its formal structure, is like a ballet or a sonata or a high drama. It is meant to be repeated in a predictable way; it has a defining structure that properly withstands an arbitrary and distorting interpretation.

When these three elements — priest, people, and ritual — stand in mutually correcting and enhancing rapport, the liturgy, in its integrity, obtains. But when, by overemphasis or underemphasis, one or more move out of this healthy, organic interdependence, the liturgy falls into corruption. In a word, these very features help us identify the characteristic abuses of the Mass: clericalism, congregationalism, and ritualism. The clericalistic abuse occurs when the role and importance of the priest are exaggerated, when the priest inserts himself too aggressively into the liturgy, turning it into a forum for his personality and the expression of his peculiar viewpoints. Mannion speaks in this context of the "talk-show host priest," a character who was unhappily prevalent in the years just after the council. This is the celebrant who chatters and jokes his way through the Mass, oblivious to its essential dynamics and to the expectations of the congregation. There is also, to be sure, a clericalism of the right. This might manifest itself in the priest who is so caught up in his own pious performance and prerogatives of station that he remains indifferent, even hostile, to the people whom he is leading in prayer.

The congregationalist abuse occurs when the people assert themselves too aggressively in the liturgical context. Distorting the meaning of their baptism and exaggerating the call for full, conscious, and active participation on the part of the laity, some people, especially in the years after the council, sought to eliminate all differentiation within the liturgical body, fostering an egalitarianism at odds with Catholic practice. In too many churches, the priest became a mere "presider," much like the president of a democratic assembly, and the ritual was changed according to the shifting whims of the congregation. Some envisioned the Mass as the creation of the people, an artifact designed for spiritual entertainment and uplift. But when priest and ritual are so manipulated or marginalized, the delicate liturgical balance is upset, and the Mass devolves into a parody of itself.

And finally, the ritualist problem emerges when the rite itself becomes too dominant. As we've seen, no Shakespearean director should distort the text of the master, but the most effective stagers of Shakespeare know how to bring the text to life, to recover it precisely through a novel interpretation. So the Mass is a living thing, to a certain degree new each time it is offered, precisely in the measure that each priest and each congregation is unique. Again, this is no license for over-experimentation; but it is an insistence that the Mass rise above the level of a museum piece, a precious but lifeless *objet d'art*. One of the ways that this ritualism manifests itself is in a sort of liturgical aestheticism. The liturgy is meant not so much to be studied as to be lived.

Thus, we lovers of the Mass want a circumincession, a reciprocal existence, of priest, people, and rite; and we want to keep at bay the shadow side of each: clericalism, congregationalism, and ritualism. In right balance, the liturgy can indeed show itself as the source and summit of the Christian life.

Part Six

Faith and Culture

BIBLICAL FAMILY VALUES
1 Samuel 1:9–28

T HERE ARE FAMILY VALUES on display in the Bible, but they're probably not the ones you'd expect. We tend to be rather sentimental in regard to families, emphasizing the importance of emotional connections and personal bonds. But the biblical authors urge us to see the "values" of a family in an entirely different way. Unlike what we've come to expect, their approach is not romantic at all, but rather harsh, blunt, and demanding.

A particularly illuminating case in point is the story of Hannah, told in the first chapter of the first book of Samuel. We are told that the childless Hannah would go every year up to the temple at Shiloh to pray, begging God that she might become pregnant. Once she was beseeching the Lord so passionately and with so many tears that the prophet Eli assumed she was intoxicated. He upbraided her: "How long will you make a drunken spectacle of yourself? Put away your wine." It would be hard to imagine a more miserable scenario for Hannah: not only is she agonizing over her unfortunate situation, but she is publicly humiliated by the leading religious authority in the temple. Displaying extraordinary courage, she stands her ground: "No, my lord, I am a woman deeply troubled; I have drunk neither wine nor strong drink, but I have been pouring out my soul before the Lord." She tells Eli precisely how she had been praying: "O Lord of hosts, if only you will look on the misery of your servant . . . and will give to your servant a male child, then I will set him before you as a nazirite until the day of his death." (A nazirite was the ancient Israelite version of a monk, someone utterly dedicated to God and God's service.)

Yahweh heard her prayer, and in due time Hannah conceived and bore a son, whom she named Samuel, meaning "desired of the Lord." And when Samuel was weaned, his mother, in fulfillment of her vow, brought him to the temple and gave him to Eli to be raised as a man of God. We know, of course, that Samuel grew to be one of the most pivotal and powerful figures in the history of Israel, playing a key role in the careers of Saul and David and setting the tone for so many of the prophets who would follow him.

Samuel was the son that his mother desired with all her heart, the child for whom she begged year after year.

When she held him for the first time in her arms, she must have felt, with special fierceness, that almost mystical connection that mothers have with their children. And yet, despite this bond, she let him go. Despite the wrenching emotions she must have experienced, she allowed him to find his mission according to the will and purpose of God.

On the feast of the Holy Family, the church invites us to read the Hannah story in tandem with the account of Mary and Joseph finding the child Jesus in the temple, and the juxtaposition is enlightening. Looking desperately for their lost son over the course of three days, enduring sleepless nights, envisioning over and again the worst possible scenarios, Mary and Joseph must have experienced the darkest of emotions. Thus, when they finally track him down in the temple precincts, debating with the elders, they are understandably exasperated. Mary chastises him: "Child, why have you treated us like this? Look, your father and I have been searching for you in great anxiety." But Jesus appears oblivious to their frantic emotions and replies with devastating brevity: "Why were you searching for me? Did you not know that I must be in my Father's house?"

Once more, despite the intense feelings of his mother, a child finds his place in the temple. In both narratives, what is being dramatically called into question is the primacy of emotion and personal feeling in determining a child's life. What matters above all, the Bible teaches over and again, is to find one's mission — and nothing, not even the strongest familial bonds, ought to obstruct that task. Sentiment, however legitimate and understandable, devolves into self-regarding sentimentality when it takes primacy over the purposes of God.

With these counterintuitive stories of Mary and Hannah in mind, let us consider a few of Jesus' own choice comments about families. When a prospective disciple asks for leave to bury his father — an act of piety as highly prized in first-century Jewish culture as it is in ours — Jesus replies with a bluntness that we could only characterize as deeply insensitive: "Let the dead bury their dead." When a woman cries out enthusiastically, "Blessed are the breasts that nursed you and the womb that bore you," Jesus fires back, "Blessed rather are those who hear the word of God and keep it." On still another occasion, when his disciples say, "Your mother and brothers are outside asking for you," Jesus replies, "Who are my mother and my brothers? Whoever does the will of God are brother and sister and mother to me." And most devastatingly: "Do not think I have come to bring peace on the earth; I have not come to bring peace, but a sword. For I have come to set a man against his father, and daughter against her mother." What could these blistering and provocative comments possibly mean? In line with the biblical principle we have been exposing, Jesus insists upon the proper prioritization of spiritual values. To listen to the word of God, to follow after the Messiah, to do the will of the Lord are the supreme goods, and they must not be compromised by, or rendered secondary to, any other good. In order to test his disciples, therefore, Jesus purposely contrasts the Gospel call to those most emotionally precious and ethically compelling values that obtain within families. Even these — especially these — must give way before the demands of God. Nowhere is this principle more succinctly summarized than in this saying of the Lord: "Whoever loves father or mother more than me is not worthy of me; and whoever loves son or daughter more than me is not worthy of me."

Given this biblical reading, it is easy enough to see what typically goes wrong with families. A father might be striving to realize his frustrated athletic or professional dreams through his son, thereby reducing his child to a means for the attainment of a self-centered end. A mother might be driving a daughter to perfection in all things, failing all the while to see that her child is collapsing under the pressure. In order to maintain a superficial peace, or simply because they're too lazy or bored to care, parents don't address the dysfunctional behavior of their children. Or a son can use his parents as a source of financial or emotional security, caring nothing for their well-being. In all of these cases, something other than the flourishing of the other is paramount; something other than divine mission — pleasure, pride, success, the working out of psychological frustration — is placed at the center of familial concern. This is precisely the manner in which families become an obstacle to God's intentions and have to be placed rather radically in question.

John Paul II said often that the family is meant to be an *ecclesiola* — a little church. This means that the family is the forum in which the worship of God is the supreme value and the discernment of mission is the supreme task. Parents should realize that their first responsibility is to shape their children not so much for worldly accomplishment but for God's work. And they should, therefore, cultivate the emotional detachment necessary to these ends — and demonstrate the quality so clearly on display in both Hannah and Mary: the willingness to let their children remain in the temple.

BEING AMERICAN,
BEING CATHOLIC
Galatians 5:1

EVERY CULTURE is evangelically ambiguous — that is to say, to some degree conducive to the preaching of the Gospel and to some degree antipathetic to it. Our American culture is no exception to this general rule; indeed, the ambiguity is particularly rich and dense in our context. America has been formed by hundreds of different influences, but the two major factors that contributed to the shaping of our culture are the rationalism of the eighteenth-century Enlightenment and Protestant Christianity. Both of these are, at the same time, deeply related to Roman Catholicism *and* stated opponents of the church. This is why being Catholic and being American has always been, to say the least, a complicated matter. I'd like to look, however briefly, at both sides of the ledger, examining one feature of the American culture that is particularly opposed to Christ's Gospel and another particularly congruent with it.

There is probably no idea that so stirs the American heart as freedom. We are, after all, the land of the free and the home of the brave. "Don't tread on me," that motto from the Revolutionary period, is one that, I imagine, most Americans would still rather readily embrace. In both high culture and popular culture, the archetype of the heroic individual who fights for his or her freedom against an oppressive institution is a favorite motif. This American conception of freedom is one whose roots can be found in the philosophers of the late Middle Ages and whose full expression occurred in the modern period. It is freedom as choice and self-determination. To be free, on this reading, is to hover above the "yes" and the "no" and to be able, without any constraint, to decide for one or the other.

But there is a much older understanding of freedom, which is on display in both classical philosophy and the Bible. This could be termed "freedom for excellence." According to this interpretation, freedom is not so much individual choice as the disciplining of desire so as to make the achievement of the good, first *possible,* and then *effortless.* For example, I became a free speaker of English — able to say pretty much whatever I want — not by arbitrarily deciding to speak as I saw fit, but by submitting myself to a whole series of disciplines, exercises, masters, and mentors. Michael Jordan became the freest man ever to play basketball, not by choosing to play according to his whim, but through a lifelong process of discipline, practice, and submission to the exigencies of the game. The first type of freedom is in a tensive relationship with law and claims to objective truth, for they will necessarily be construed as limitations on the range of choice; but the second type of freedom positively requires the law and the good, for it finds itself in surrendering to them.

The difference between these two kinds of freedom is not merely abstract. Look at the decision of the U.S. Supreme Court in 1992, in the matter of *Casey v. Planned Parenthood*. Trying to bolster their earlier judgment on reproductive questions and abortion articulated in *Roe v. Wade*, the justices ruled that it belongs to the very nature of liberty to determine the meaning of one's own life, of existence, and of the universe. This is a nearly perfect expression of modern freedom. Contrast this Supreme Court ruling with two statements from the letters of St. Paul. In his first letter to the Corinthians, Paul sums up his Gospel with these words: "It is for freedom that Christ has set you free"; and in his letter to the Romans, he presents himself, baldly enough, as "Paul, a slave of Christ Jesus." This juxtaposition — non-sensical

193

on modern grounds — expresses beautifully the correlation between freedom and truth that the Bible takes for granted. The sharp contrast between these two views of liberty make the proclamation of biblical Christianity problematic in our American cultural framework.

There are also positive dimensions of our American culture. I would invite you to drift back in imagination to a stuffy Philadelphia boardinghouse in the sweltering summer of 1776, where a young Virginia lawyer was composing a rather important document. In the opening paragraph of the Declaration of Independence, Thomas Jefferson wrote, "We hold these truths to be self-evident, that all men are created equal and are endowed by their Creator with certain inalienable rights...." If someone had suggested to Plato, Aristotle, or Cicero that it is self-evident that all people are fundamentally equal and endowed with inviolable rights, he would have been met with a very puzzled look. For the classical philosophers, precisely the opposite seemed self-evident. People, they felt, are rather radically different in matters such as intelligence, beauty, physical prowess, creativity, and moral excellence, and a frank acknowledgment of these inequalities appeared to be the prerequisite for right political order. Hence in Plato's *Republic*, we hear that the just city will emerge only when the best people rule, the second-best people serve in the military, and the less intellectually and morally endowed take care of menial tasks. And in Aristotle's *Politics,* we learn that only a tiny handful of the intellectually and economically elite are allowed to participate in public life. Equality and fundamental rights are not even on the radar screen.

So how did Jefferson come by these convictions? The clue is found in two words in his text that we usually pass over in haste, perhaps seeing them as little more than pious decoration: "created" and "Creator." All people, Jefferson implies, are equal in the measure that they are equally children of God. They have rights, further-more, in the measure that they have been granted them by their Creator. Loved into existence and destined for eternal life, they are subjects of inviolable dignity and have a legitimate claim to life, liberty, and the pursuit of happiness. Without the clear reference to the Creator God, Jefferson's political convictions become, to put it mildly, somewhat less than self-evident. And this was amply proven by the totalitarianisms of the last century. Both Nazism and Communism demonstrated that the marginalization or outright denial of God leads, in very short order, to the egregious violation of human rights and dignity. In 1981, John Paul II was speaking to a crowd of his fellow Poles concerning basic human rights. In the midst of his address, the people began to chant, "We want God; we want God." Those who were there testify that this cry went on for seventeen minutes. What John Paul's audience sensed, at his suggestion, was the link between the affirmation of human rights and the affirmation of the God who alone can truly ground them. Therefore, in this regard, Catholics can vigorously and unapologetically embrace the political ideals upon which the nation is founded, for they cohere beautifully with some of the most elemental convictions of the Bible. We are, indeed, one nation under God.

So what is the right attitude of the Catholic vis-à-vis our American culture? It is one of affection, conditioned by critical intelligence. Catholics should take a good, honest look at the American culture and assimilate what they can, while resisting what they must. Can we be both Americans and Catholics? Yes, but we must be Catholics first.

"I SAW NO TEMPLE
IN THE CITY...."
Revelation 21:22

I F YOU WERE TO CONDUCT a routine search on the
Internet for the phrase "book of Revelation," millions of sites would appear for your perusal. Among the
best-selling novels of all time are the contemporary *Left
Behind* series, based upon a literalist interpretation of the
book of Revelation. The final book of the Bible has, for
centuries, fascinated readers, and there has perhaps been
no age more captivated by it than our own. How are we
to approach this strange and unnerving text? The book of
the Apocalypse (to use its older and somehow more chill-
ing title) is not so much a literal prediction of the end
times or an ancient literary puzzle, as a densely textured
symbolic and narrative presentation of the meaning of
the dying and rising of Jesus Christ. What struck all
of the first great Christian authors — John, Paul, Peter,
and the rest — is that the Paschal Mystery signaled the

end of the world as we know it and the beginning of a new order of things.

Ends and beginnings are always painful. When an old structure gives way and a new one emerges (whether we are speaking of the psychological, the physical, or the metaphysical dimension), sparks tend to fly and foundations tend to rock. Thus the author of Revelation vividly describes God's judgment on the old world: plagues, famine, warfare, fire, insects, earthquake, and avenging angels are visited upon the earth, producing a thoroughgoing destruction, or better, a cleansing. All of this calamity represents, finally, the author's assessment of the power of Christ's cross. Whatever contributed to the death of the Son of Man — selfishness, worldly power, ambition, violence, scapegoating, and stupidity — is under judgment and is therefore passing away. The powers that had heretofore ruled the earth are being cleared away, much as an old building is smashed to rubble and removed in order to make way for new construction.

After telling us of the destruction, the author of Revelation begins, in lyrical language, to evoke a new order, to envision a manner of earthly existence congruent with God's designs. Hence, as the text comes to its climax, we hear of the arrival of a new, eschatological Jerusalem, coming down from heaven as a bride. This is a symbol of the world as God wants it to be, and therefore this part of the book of the Apocalypse is a meditation on the power of the resurrection of Jesus from the dead, the act by which God the Father is making all things new.

The new Jerusalem is brilliantly evoked: "The wall is built of jasper, while the city is pure gold, clear as glass. The foundations of the wall of the city are adorned with every jewel...and the twelve gates are twelve pearls." But the most extraordinary detail is this one: "I saw no temple in the city, for its temple is the Lord God the Almighty and the Lamb." This is, to say the least, counterintuitive. The temple was the chief attraction and raison d'être of the earthly Jerusalem, its economic, cultural, and of course religious center. It was precisely because of the temple that Jerusalem was uniquely the holy city, God's dwelling place on earth. So one would think that, if any building was essential to the godly order of the heavenly Jerusalem, it would be a house of worship. Yet we are explicitly told that there is no temple in the gleaming city with the gates of pearl.

Paul Tillich gives us a clue to the interpretation of this symbol. He says that the surest sign of the effects of original sin in the world is the presence of a church house alongside the courthouse and the playhouse, next to the sports arena and the places of business. What he means is that, in our sin, we have tended to make "religion" one concern among many, a carefully sequestered form of life that has no real impact on the whole of life. But this, he implies, is untenable for Christians. God, as Thomas Aquinas argued, is not *a* being, not one thing among many, but rather that which sustains the whole universe the way a singer sustains a song. But this means that all things are effected by God, rooted and grounded in him, and therefore ordered finally to him. Thus, in the properly ordered city, there would, as St. John saw, be no separate temple, no single place of worship, because the whole of the city would be suffused with God — the whole of the city would be a place where God is worshiped.

Now what does this look like concretely? A lawyer might do his work out of love for money or status (and there is nothing wrong with those motives in themselves), but he will lawyer effectively and with moral purpose only when his efforts are rooted in an unconditioned passion for justice. But God is nothing other than justice itself. Therefore, when the lawyer is most a lawyer, his whole professional life becomes an act of worship, because it is suffused with God's meaning and purpose. A physician or nurse or medical technician might do her work to make a living, but she will do it well and with spiritual vigor only when she grounds it in an unconditioned desire to love the patients she serves. But God is nothing but love itself. Therefore, when the doctor is most a doctor, she engages in an act of worship and becomes a vehicle for the realization of God's designs. A writer, a journalist, a playwright might craft words for the sake of titillating the crowd, but he knows that his work will have enduring value only to the degree that he is seized by an unconditioned desire to speak the truth. But God is the Truth itself. Therefore the properly ordered journalist or poet is, perhaps despite himself, giving praise to God. A singer might perform for the thrill of popular approbation, but she will really find her voice only inasmuch as she falls unconditionally in love with beauty. But God is nothing other than the beautiful itself. And thus when she sings as fully and perfectly as she can, she is, consciously or not, a member of the chorus in the heavenly Jerusalem.

Modern philosophers, imagining God as a distant supreme being, invented the secular realm — that is to say, the dimension of existence essentially untouched by God. They furthermore conceived religion as a private "spiritual" preoccupation having nothing to do with the demands, efforts, and vicissitudes of everyday life. This privatized (and thus harmless) religion they then condescended to "tolerate" as part of their political program. But biblical religion can have no truck with this sort of modernism. God is not a supreme being, but rather

201

the energy in which all things "live and move and have their being," and there is, finally, no blandly neutral arena of life that God refuses to touch. Therefore a private religion — enshrined in one tame institution among many — is indeed, as Tillich saw, a sign of sin and an affront to the true God. In the heavenly Jerusalem, God invades the whole of life.

Allow me to make some practical recommendations in regard to resisting the modern tyranny and refusing to privatize your faith. Let the language of the Bible be on your lips naturally, spontaneously, unabashedly, especially when you are about your professional business. Put a symbol of your religious convictions — a crucifix, an icon, a picture of your patron saint — in your place of work, where it can be noticed. Place a biblical verse as the screen saver on your computer; wear a sign of your faith on your person. Finally, and above all, prayerfully relate all that you are doing in your professional life to the demands and purposes of God. Ask the creator of all things fully to take possession of your career as a lawyer, a physician, a parent, a teacher, an architect, or an engineer. In all these ways, you become, increasingly, a citizen of the heavenly Jerusalem — and a threat to the fallen world.

THE LESSONS OF
NEHEMIAH
Nehemiah 8:1–8

T HE BOOK OF NEHEMIAH is not one of the better
known books of the Bible, but the central lesson
contained in it is, I think, specially relevant for our times.
Nehemiah was a Jew of the fifth century B.C. who was
serving as cup-bearer to Artaxerxes, the king of Persia.
The Jewish nation, we recall, had been conquered by the
Babylonians in 587 B.C., and the people had been carried off into exile. Subsequently, the Babylonians were
overrun by the Persians, and under the Persian mon-
archs Cyrus, Xerxes, and Artaxerxes Jews were gradually
allowed to return to their homeland. As the narrative
of the book gets under way, Nehemiah makes a request of the benign king that he serves: "May I return
to Jerusalem and help to repair the capital city of my
people?" Graciously, the king accedes. Accordingly, the
book of Nehemiah is about the restoration of Israel,

the reconstitution of a city and a nation after a time of decay.

Upon his arrival in Jerusalem, Nehemiah engaged in a careful inspection of the city walls. He noticed, to his alarm, that they remained in the same pitiful condition in which they had been left by the Babylonians: breached, broken down, and destroyed by fire. With energy and clarity of purpose, he then drew the demoralized stragglers and refugees together and told them: "You see the trouble we are in, how Jerusalem lies in ruins with its gates burned. Come, let us rebuild the walls of Jerusalem, so that we may no longer suffer disgrace." The next several chapters of the book of Nehemiah are dedicated to a description of this massive rebuilding project. Beams and bolts are assembled, doors and gates are fixed, pools are cleansed, and homes are repaired. In the ancient world, walls were of decisive importance, for without them, a city was entirely vulnerable to enemy attacks and to infiltration by less than savory figures. The wall was the principal means by which a town protected its territorial and moral integrity, and this is precisely why the destruction of the wall to the holy city so infuriated Nehemiah and roused him to such exertion.

Walls, which separate inside from outside, which define and delimit, which keep in and keep out, are hence symbolic of identity — both personal and communal.

Porous and compromised boundaries lead to a flimsy sense of self and community. Several generations ago, in this country, Catholics were a fairly well-defined people, characterized by certain very definite practices (no meat on Fridays, novenas, rosaries, frequent confession) and beliefs (the Trinity, the spiritual significance of Mary and the saints, the authority of the pope, to name just a few), which distinguished them from other ethnic and religious groups. What followed from this definition was a corporate cohesiveness, a strength of character, and a clarity of mission and purpose. In the years following the Second Vatican Council, the church rather radically accommodated itself to modernity, embracing the mores and beliefs of the secular culture, emphasizing inclusivity and openness to other perspectives.

Having come of age during that immediate post-conciliar period, I can testify that the church, at that time, often assumed an apologizing, hand-wringing posture and tended to bring its beliefs and practices before the bar of the culture for evaluation. Much of this, of course, was justified through appeal to Pope John XXIII's famous conciliar image of "opening the windows" of the medieval church in order to let in the fresh air of modernity. Now, whatever John XXIII meant by that trope, we can, with Nehemiah in mind, add this clarification: he might have urged us to open the windows, but he certainly didn't tell us to tear down the walls. This elimination of the defining marks, however, this rendering porous of the walls of Catholicism, is precisely what happened in too many circles after the council. And it led to the same problem that Nehemiah noticed long ago in regard to Jerusalem: a loss of integrity and moral purpose. One way to interpret the papacy of John Paul II is according to the pattern of Nehemiah: a shoring up of the walls of Catholicism so that the identity of the church could be strengthened.

Mind you, neither Israel nor the church of Jesus Christ is meant to be a sect, crouching defensively against the world. The ultimate purpose of God's chosen people is, as Isaiah saw, to be a light to the nations, the salt of the earth, the agent by which the world is drawn into the kingdom of God. Hans Urs von Balthasar was quite right to speak in the years just before the council of the "razing of the bastions" of the church, that is to say, the breaking down of the barriers that kept the church from letting out its transformative energy. This brings us into the heart of a paradox: the church can perform its mission of world transformation effectively if and only if it has a clear sense of its identity. If and only if it attends diligently to its own walls will it be able to bring its distinctive mode of thought and practice to the wider society. We resolve this paradox far too easily when we say that since we are meant to evangelize the world, we should imitate the world and its style. Robert Frost articulated the proper tension memorably when he famously observed that "good fences make good neighbors." The church must know who she is before she can undertake her proper mission of telling the world what it ought to be.

In the eighth chapter of the book of Nehemiah, after the description of the upbuilding of the city, we find an account of what Israel did behind its newly constituted walls. The entire people — from the elders to those children old enough to understand — gathered together, and they listened to Ezra the priest as he proclaimed the Torah to them. They stood, the Scripture tells us, from early morning until midday and took in the law and its interpretation. And you think that you listen to long homilies! This ancient story is reminding us that Israel was a people formed by a definite set of narratives, practices, and laws. We, the New Israel, are determined, in a similar way, by the stories of creation, the fall, the promise of the Messiah; we are ordered by the exhortations of the prophets and the commands of the Sermon on the Mount; we are illumined by the resurrection of Jesus from the dead and the emergence, against all odds, of the church.

If we don't hear these stories and laws, we rather quickly forget who we are. In this regard, we church-people are like a group of kids who become baseball players through a whole series of exercises, drills, moves, stories, and commands, which effectively place baseball in their bodies and minds. Or we are like a bevy of immigrants who are assimilated into the American way of being, moving, acting, deciding, and speaking, through a lengthy process of cultural formation. Stanley Hauerwas, a devoted pacifist, has nevertheless spoken admiringly of the manner in which the military academies and training centers manage a thorough transformation of the young people who come to them. When they are through with boot camp or basic training, these young people look, speak, think, and act like soldiers. They know in their bones that they have entered into a distinctive community with clear boundaries and demands. In light of practices outlined in the book of Nehemiah, we can see why it's far from a minor problem that 70 percent of Catholics absent themselves from Sunday Mass. Trying to become a person of the church without attending the liturgy, receiving the Eucharist, and hearing the word of God is about as contraindicated as trying to become a baseball player by staying away from practice and ignoring the basic disciplines and rules of the game.

208

And therefore, this distant figure, Nehemiah, the governor of Judea and the rebuilder of the walls of the holy city, speaks as a prophet to our time, when an exaggerated inclusiveness and accommodation have led us toward a certain self-forgetfulness. Let us, then, like the Israelites of Nehemiah's time, gather with joy and purpose to rebuild the walls.

"WHAT IS TRUTH?"

John 18:37–19:11

O NE ISSUE our present pope finds extremely important is the relationship between classical Christianity and modern democracy. He has written extensively on this topic over the last thirty years, and it
continues to preoccupy him as pope. Here is the nub
of the problem as Benedict XVI sees it. In the wake of
the great totalitarianisms of the twentieth century, many
theorists of democracy have held that any claim to absolute truth is inimical to the exercise of real freedom.
Whenever a group within a given society says that it
knows, through divine revelation or political intuition,
what is true and good for everyone, that group becomes
a threat to the rest of the community. Almost inevitably,
the argument goes, the assertion of a transcendent truth
slides into intolerance and, finally, violence. Though, to
be sure, individuals and sects can legitimately maintain
their truth in a private manner, they cannot be allowed

to impose it on the community as a whole. Thus, as far as an authentic democracy is concerned, "truth," in the public sense, should be simply a function of the decision of the majority, a result of the ever-evolving consensus of the people.

One can find versions of this teaching in the extremely influential political philosophies of John Rawls, Richard Rorty, and Jürgen Habermas, and their interpretation of the rapport between transcendent truth and democracy has been confirmed in the minds of many by the events of September 11. Thus the dilemma emerges: is it really possible to be, at the same time, a committed advocate of democracy and a believer in a revealed and non-negotiable religious truth?

In order to bring this issue into sharper relief, Pope Benedict cites the curious biblical exegesis offered by the Austrian philosopher Hans Kelsen. In his writings on democracy, Kelsen invites us to reflect on the conversation between Jesus and Pontius Pilate as presented in the Gospel of John. When Jesus tells the Roman governor that he has come to testify to the truth, Pilate answers, with a sort of world-weary skepticism, "What is truth?" Kelsen suggests that Pilate is not so much cynical as canny. His is the voice of someone who has seen the destructiveness produced by claims to religious certitude and who is therefore wary in the extreme of this

211

proud man standing before him asserting himself to be the witness to "truth." Pontius Pilate, in short, is the prototype of the modern democrat. Moreover, Kelsen argues, Pilate has the courage of his convictions. Though he might have suspected that Jesus was innocent of the charges against him, he turned the determination of his fate over to the people, allowing the assembled crowd to vote either for Jesus or for Barabbas. Finally, having heard the *vox populi*, Pilate appropriately washed his hands of the matter, signaling that, despite his personal feelings, he was willing to go along with the stated consensus of the majority. Kelsen approves of Pilate as the avatar of a government properly skeptical and relativistic in regard to claims of ultimate truth, one based, as a consequence, not on what is purported to be the objective good, but rather on correct democratic procedures.

There is, Pope Benedict contends, a more convincing way to read that passage from the Gospel of John. We notice, first, that Jesus never questions the legitimacy of Pilate's political authority. Jesus was not a social revolutionary, summoning Israel in the manner of a Zealot to eliminate the Roman presence. In fact, when Pilate, frustrated by Jesus' silence, said, "Do you not know that I have power to release you and power to crucify you," Jesus did not deny that Pilate had that power. But he added something of great significance: "You would have no power over me unless it had been given to you from above." The authority that Pilate legitimately exercises comes, Jesus implies, not from the consensus of the governed or from the shifting convictions of the crowd, but rather from God, from that transcendent source of goodness and truth that grounds and contextualizes all valid political judgments. The Truth — which in a supreme irony, is standing personally before Pilate — is the norm and criterion of right government and can never become itself conditioned either by the decisions of the government or the vote of the majority. And this is why the Pilate who turned the fate of Jesus over to the whim of the mob is hardly a model of healthy democracy, but rather a corrupt coward.

These competing readings of the Jesus-Pilate conversation provide a neat template for Pope Benedict's resolution of the question under consideration. Freedom is indeed a great and abiding value within a democratic polity, but real freedom must be maintained in constant correlation to the truth, lest it devolve into libertinism. The free decisions of a democratic society — mediated politically by the elected government — must take place within the context of a network of truths and moral values that are not themselves subject to vote. We may indeed determine freely which prudential means are most apt for the realization of our collective goals, but the ends themselves are not a matter of deliberation — for if they were, the cohesiveness and moral purpose of the society as such would dissipate. If we look closely at modern democracies, we can find these transcendent and non-negotiable moral principles articulated in terms of inviolable human rights. Thus, as we saw, we find the rights to "life, liberty, and the pursuit of happiness" defended in Thomas Jefferson's prologue to the Declaration of Independence, as well as the unambiguous statement that these prerogatives have been "endowed by [our] Creator." What Jefferson implies here is that the decisions of the American democracy should always take place within the framework provided by these moral absolutes, which are known, not through the consensus of the governed, but through a sort of mystical intuition: "We hold these truths to be self-evident." It can never be the case, therefore, that human rights themselves become a matter of debate. When this relationship between moral context and prudential decision making is properly understood, the pope concludes, then the "problem" of democracy and claims to transcendent truth substantially dissolves.

Let us return to the beginning of the conversation between Jesus and the Roman governor. Prompted by his concern for social order, Pilate asked Jesus whether he is a king, which is to say, a threat to the Roman polity. After clarifying that his kingship has nothing to do with the maintaining of order through violence and conquest ("my kingdom is not of this world"), Jesus subtly correlated his authentic kingship with truth — and this is the key. Jesus is not interested in usurping Pilate's authority by becoming a king in the manner of David or Solomon and taking over the practical management of the state. But he is indeed interested in asserting his moral and spiritual sovereignty over any and all of the decisions that Pilate should make as governor. He is indeed claiming that whatever authority Pilate has comes, not simply from his Roman superiors, but ultimately from "above," from a transcendent king.

And this distinction provides the solution to the puzzle of "church and state" questions that bedevil us today. At its best, the church expresses no interest in meddling in the practical affairs of government. No priest, bishop, or pope should interfere in the details of composing a bill or organizing a committee hearing or concocting a legislative strategy. But the church ought very much to articulate in a public way the moral context for any and all government activity, and it should indeed raise its prophetic voice when practical politics militates against the rights, freedom, and dignity of the individual. This is the right way to proclaim the Kingship of Christ and the sovereignty of transcendent truth over political process.

EPHPHATHA!

Mark 7:31–37

IN THE SEVENTH CHAPTER of the Gospel of Mark, we find the moving account of Jesus' healing of a man who is unable to speak or to hear. As is always the case with these narratives of miraculous cures, we have to look at both the surface meaning and the deeper meaning. One of the relatively few things that even the most skeptical of New Testament critics agree upon is that Jesus had a reputation as a healer and wonder-worker. Certainly a major reason why crowds followed him and bothered to listen to his teaching was that they were attracted by the prospect of a miracle. Thus it is safe to say that this story — so marked by psychological perception and attention to curious detail — concerns a real event in the ministry of Jesus. But since, as Augustine pointed out, Jesus is the Word made flesh, every one of his actions is also a word, that is to say, a revelation of some abiding and universal spiritual truth. So let us endeavor to decipher some of the symbolic meanings hidden in the story.

As the narrative commences, Jesus is making his way into the Decapolis, the region of the "ten cities" on the southeastern side of the Sea of Galilee. These ten towns were very much under Hellenistic influence and therefore marked by a certain religious syncretism, blendings of Jewish and Gentile beliefs. A deaf man is brought to the Lord. Is it surprising, if we pursue our symbolic reading, that in this religiously mixed area there would be someone deaf to the Word of God? Hearing is, of course, a major scriptural motif, for the God of the Bible speaks, and his speech goes out to a people who are meant to hearken to his voice. The young Samuel, at the prompting of Eli the priest, says in response to the inviting voice of Yahweh, "Speak, Lord, your servant is listening." The prophets are channels of the divine word, and they continually urge Israel not to be dull and inattentive. The central statement of Israelite faith, the interpretive key to the entire Old Testament, is the *Sh'ma:* "Hear, O Israel, the Lord your God is Lord alone." And St. Paul tells the Christian church at Rome that "faith comes from hearing." Therefore, this deaf man, brought before Jesus, stands for all of us who do not or cannot hear the Word of God, all of us who have grown oblivious to it or lost the capacity to discern it with clarity.

What makes someone today unable to hear God's word? Consider, first, the incredible variety of voices and sounds competing for our attention. Technology has made readily available to us voices from TVs, iPods, BlackBerries, boom-boxes, radios, movies, telephones, and computers; and from these various media, we hear, in their infinite variety, politicians, pop stars, advertisers, preachers, musicians, commentators, clowns, and fools. Elijah experienced Yahweh as a tiny, whispering sound, and John the Baptist heard the Lord's voice in the still-ness of the desert. How can we be anything but deaf to divine speech, surrounded as we are by such a relentless cacophony?

Moreover, more and more of us are staying away from church and growing, consequently, increasingly ignorant of the Bible. A few years ago, I was a visiting profes-sor at a major Catholic university. In the course of my lecturing, I would regularly refer to biblical passages — Job, the woman at the well, the parables of Jesus — and I was continually amazed how often these very bright young people, almost all of whom were from a Catholic background, were oblivious to the Scripture. And this is by no means a problem unique to Catholics. The bibli-cal literacy that could be assumed in the nineteenth and early twentieth century is no longer present in the popu-lar culture. Just think how blithely Melville, Hawthorne,

Faulkner, and Hemingway could assume that their audience was conversant with the Bible; now their biblical allusions have to be carefully explained even to an alert reader.

A third problem is, if I can put it this way, a kind of tone-deafness in regard to the Word of God. Some people can hear musical notes, but they are incapable of discriminating clearly and consistently between a melody that is in tune with the accompaniment and one that is off-key. They hear "music," but they can't discern between relatively good and bad tones. Something similar obtains in regard to the things of the spirit. There is an awful lot of "religious" speech on offer in the culture today, but too many of us are tin-eared when it comes to telling the difference between authentic biblical religion and other varieties. The pronouncements of the pope, the speeches of the Dalai Lama, the cultural assessments offered by television evangelists, and the psychological truisms presented by avatars of the New Age can all sound vaguely "religious" or "spiritual" to those tone deaf to the nuances of religious speech.

Now the man brought to Jesus suffers, not only from deafness, but from that inevitable concomitant of deafness, the inability to speak clearly. If a person is unable properly to hear sounds, she remains incapable, obviously, of reproducing those sounds in her own speech.

This physical dynamic is precisely reproduced in the spiritual order: deafness to the Word of God results in a severe incapacity to speak that Word articulately and with any convincing power. How many Catholics today can speak the Word of God with clarity and confidence? How many of us become tongue-tied when people ask us what we believe or pose a pointed question about the faith? Many Catholics complain that they feel incapable of effectively evangelizing, because they simply don't know enough about the Scripture, theology, and the teachings of the church. This awkwardness of speech flows from the deafness we just explored.

So what does Jesus do with the deaf and dumb man? Mark tells us that "he took him off by himself away from the crowd." We saw something very similar in Mark's story of the healing of a blind man: Jesus led the man away from the village, and when he had cured him, he told him not to return to the town. The crowd, as we hinted above, is a large part of the problem. The raucous voices of so many, the prevalence of the received wisdom, the insistent bray of the advertising culture, the confusing Babel of competing spiritualities — all of it makes us deaf to God's word. And therefore, we have to be moved away, to a place of silence and communion. Jesus draws us, accordingly, into his space, the space of the church. There, away from the crowd, we can immerse ourselves in the rhythm of the liturgy, listen avidly to the Scripture, study the theological tradition, watch at close quarters the moves of holy people, take in the beauty of sacred art and architecture. There we can hear.

Here is how Mark describes the actual cure: "Jesus put his finger in the man's ears and, spitting, touched his tongue; then he looked up to heaven and groaned, and said to him, '*Ephphatha!*' ['Be opened']." Scholars tell us that spitting and touching of the tongue were gestures typically employed by healers in Jesus' day. But I find the other details most intriguing. Looking up to his Father and inserting his fingers into the man's ears, Jesus establishes, as it were, an electrical current, running from the Father, through the Son, into the suffering man. He literally plugs him in to the divine energy, compelling him to hear the Word. And how wonderful is that groaning "*Ephphatha,*" one of only three times that the Gospel writers preserve Jesus' original Aramaic speech. Once the man is opened to the divine Word, he begins to speak clearly. So would we, away from the cacophonous crowd and plugged into the dynamism of Jesus Christ and his church. If you want to speak the Word persuasively, listen attentively!

Index of Names

Anselm, 68
Aquinas, Thomas, 4, 35, 39, 51, 68, 76–78, 80–81, 106–7, 110, 132, 137, 141, 172, 175, 200
Aristotle, 38, 149, 194, 195
Augustine, 4, 48–49, 51, 101–3, 106, 111, 166, 216

Balthasar, Hans Urs von, 81, 176, 206
Barenboim, Daniel, 136–37
Barth, Karl, 4, 70
Belloc, Hilaire, 136
Benedict XVI, 150, 210–14. See also Ratzinger, Joseph
Bernard of Clairvaux, 4
Bossuet, Jacques-Benigne, 4
Buddha, 53, 146

Caravaggio, 127–30
Charlemagne, 151
Chesterton, G. K., 13, 151
Chrysostom, John, 51
Cicero, 149, 194
Clapton, Eric, 137
Clark, Kenneth, 68

Colson, Charles, 132–33
Coltrane, John, 136
Confucius, 53, 146

Dante, 51, 89
Day, Dorothy, 27, 143–44
Descartes, René, 120
Dostoevsky, Fyodor, 32

Eckhart, Meister, 4
Einstein, Albert, 38–39, 41

Faulkner, William, 219
Favre, Brett, 108
Feuerbach, Ludwig, 18–21
Francis of Assisi, 26, 140
Freud, Sigmund, 19, 20, 121
Frost, Robert, 207

George, Francis, 150–51
Gregory the Great, 106
Guardini, Romano, 176

Habermas, Jürgen, 211
Haight, Roger, 52, 53
Hauerwas, Stanley, 208

Hawthorne, Nathaniel, 23–24, 218–19
Hawthorne, Rose, 23–27
Hefner, Hugh, 120
Hemingway, Ernest, 58, 219
Henry VIII, 109
Hitler, Adolf, 151

Irenaeus, 135

Jefferson, Thomas, 18, 194–95, 214
Jerome, 51
Jeter, Derek, 173
John XXIII, 205–6
John of the Cross, 17
John Paul II, 36, 69, 190, 195–96, 206
Jordan, Michael, 193

Kant, Immanuel, 60
Kelsen, Hans, 211–12
Kennedy, John F., 2
Kierkegaard, Søren, 94–96
King, Martin Luther, Jr., 2
Kolbe, Maximilian, 109

Lathrop, John, 24–26
Lenin, Vladimir, 21
Lincoln, Abraham, 53
Locke, John, 18, 36, 37
Lonergan, Bernard, 38, 39

Lubac, Henri de, 176
Luther, Martin, 112

Mannion, M. Francis, 176–80
Mao Tse-Tung, 21
Marx, Karl, 18–21
Mary Alphonsa, 26
Maurin, Peter, 140–45
Mello, Anthony de, 163
Melville, Herman, 218–19
Merton, Thomas, 130–31, 179
Michel, Virgil, 176
Michelangelo, 51, 119, 128
More, Thomas, 109
Mozart, Amadeus, 118
Muhammad, 146

Napoleon, 151
Newman, John Henry, 4, 37–40, 51, 178
Newton, Isaac, 18, 38
Nixon, Richard, 132

Origen, 4, 33

Padre Pio, 78
Pierce, Franklin, 23
Pius IX, 24
Plato, 54, 113, 120, 121, 149, 194
Plotinus, 120
Prometheus, 135
Pythagoras, 149

Ratzinger, Joseph, 13, 176. *See* also Benedict XVI
Rawls, John, 211
Rorty, Richard, 211

Sade, Marquis de, 120
Sax, Leonard, 115–16
Schillebeeckx, Edward, 52, 53
Shakespeare, William, 118
Sheen, Fulton, 2, 3
Sokolowski, Robert, 178
Stalin, Joseph, 21, 151

Tanner, Kathryn, 11
Teresa of Avila, 51
Teresa of Calcutta, 26, 36, 51, 78
Therese of Lisieux, 108
Tillich, Paul, 3, 35, 60, 199–200, 202

Vidal, Gore, 87–88, 90

Watson, Mary, 25
Williams, Tennessee, 88
Wright, N. T., 54

Also by Robert Barron

AND NOW I SEE...
A Theology of Transformation

"The reading of this book is like a guided visit to some vast treasure house where we are invited to explore the rich heritage of Christian thought. With the eyes of artists and the insights of poets, we walk with saints, philosophers, and theologians, challenged to move from blindness and fear to freedom and vision through Christ. At the end of the visit, we realize that we have actually begun, with renewed energy and enthusiasm, a journey — a pilgrimage — along the path of faith and conversion, trust, and love. This is a book 'for all seasons'!"

— Agnes Cunningham, SSCM, theologian
and author of *Prayer: Personal and Liturgical*

"Robert Barron, an inspired writer, illuminates the teachings of 'the great tradition,' showing how they coalesce with the best literary witnesses to liberate us to our true selves. His reflections range from the philosophical to the poetic, themselves inspired by the riches of the tradition they unearth."

— David B. Burrell, CSC, Hesburgh Professor of
Philosophy and Theology, University of Notre Dame

0-8245-1753-9, paperback